Treasures of the
UFFIZI
FLORENCE

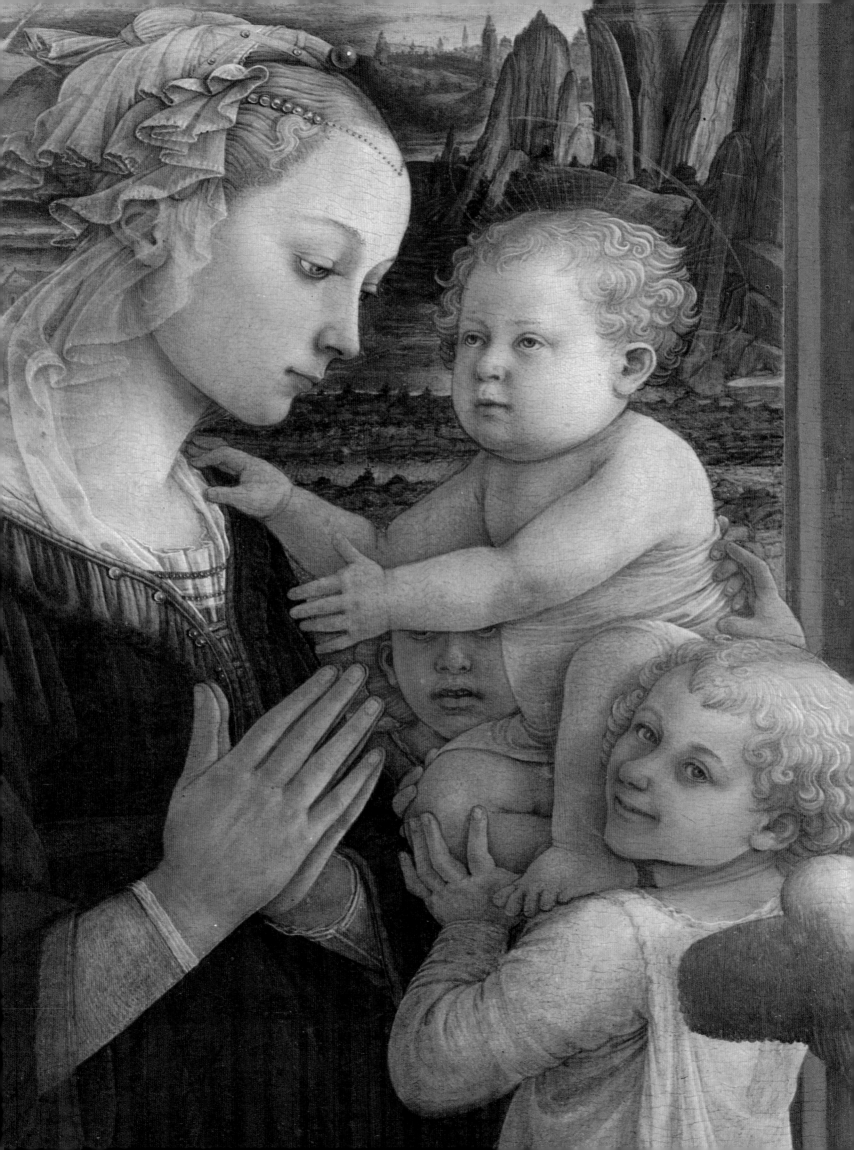

Treasures of the
UFFIZI
FLORENCE

Abbeville Press Publishers
New York   London   Paris

Front cover: Detail of Sandro Botticelli, *Primavera,* 1477–80. See page 42.
Back cover: Michelangelo Buonarroti, *The Holy Family (The Doni Tondo),* 1504. See page 12.
Frontispiece: Detail of Fra Filippo Lippi, *Madonna and Child with Two Angels,* c. 1464. See page 29.
Page 5: Raphael (1483–1520). *Pope Leo X with Cardinals Giulio de' Medici and Luigi de' Rossi,* c. 1518. Oil on wood, 60½ x 46½ in. (155.5 x 119.5 cm).
Page 6: Detail of Giuseppe Zocchi (1711–1767), *View of the Uffizi,* n.d.

EDITOR: ABIGAIL ASHER
DESIGNER: LAURA LINDGREN
PRODUCTION MANAGER: LOU BILKA

All photographs by Paolo Tosi, Summerfield Press Limited, Bagno a Ripoli (Florence), except those on the following pages, which are by Takashi Okamura: 12, 29 bottom.

First edition
10 9 8 7 6 5 4 3 2 1

Library of Congress Cataloging-in-Publication Data
Galleria degli Uffizi
   Treasures of the Uffizi Florence.
   p. cm.
   Includes index.
   ISBN 0-7892-0234-4
   1. Painting—Italy—Florence—Catalogs. 2. Galleria degli Uffizi—Catalogs I. Title.
N2570.A755 1996
759.94'074'4551—dc20   96-12131

Contents

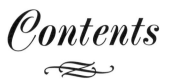

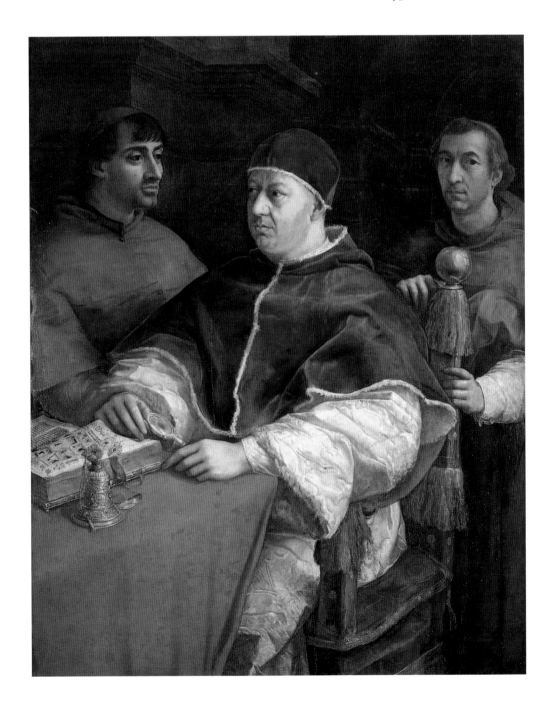

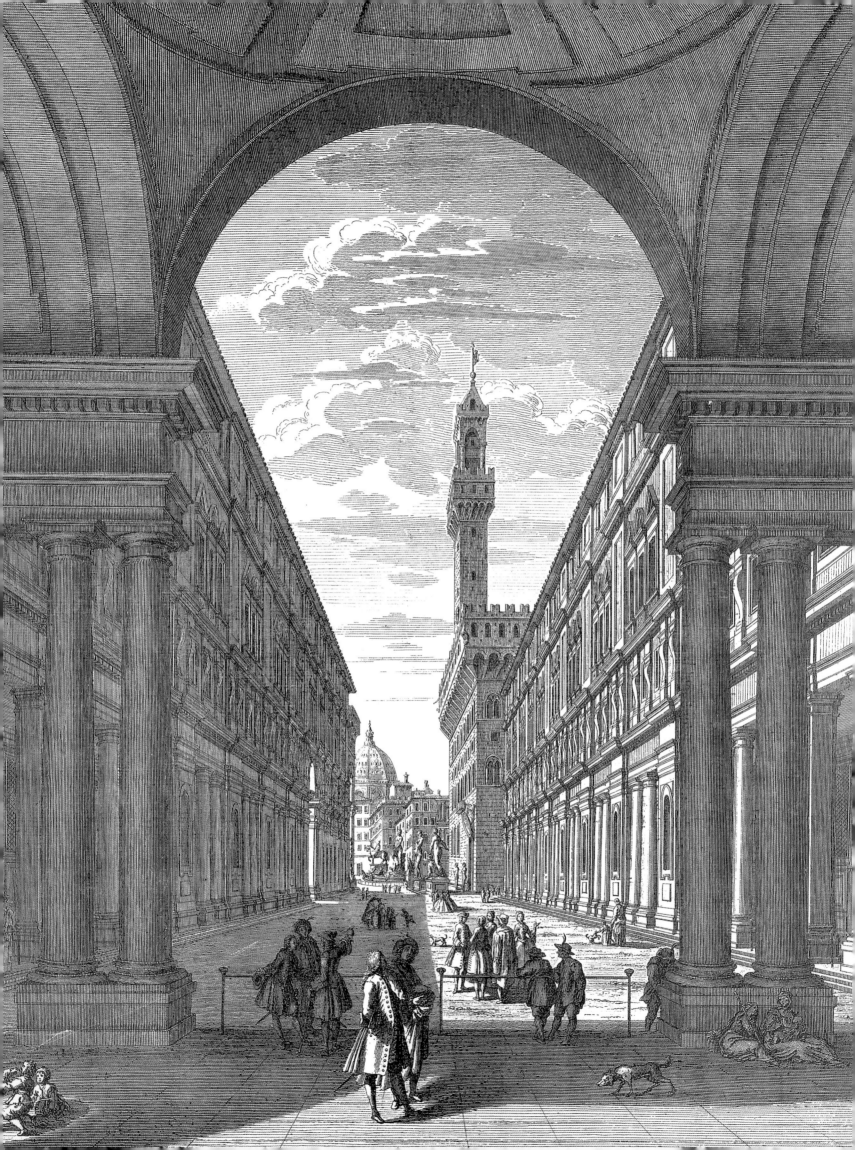

Introduction

IN THIS VOLUME ARE REPRODUCED the best paintings from the Uffizi Gallery, among them the most famous works of the Italian Renaissance, which made Florence and Tuscany famous throughout the world. The history of the Uffizi reflects its close relationship with the city of Florence.

The Uffizi was the first European museum assembled to serve purposes that were not only—or at least not essentially—private. When the original nucleus of the collection took form, the great palace that was to house it and eventually give it its name already existed. Cosimo I de' Medici (1519–1574), who became grand duke of Tuscany in 1569, had the palace built by Giorgio Vasari (1511–1574). It was originally made to house the administrative offices (*uffizi*) of the new grand duchy, for Cosimo, whose family dynasty was to rule in Tuscany until 1737, wanted to build his state upon a solid bureaucratic foundation. The new centralized form of the Florentine government was physically demonstrated by the Uffizi's connection on one side, by way of a bridge, to the Palazzo Vecchio, ancient seat of the city government, and on the other side, by way of a long passageway (known as the Vasari Corridor), to the Pitti, the grand ducal palace.

An elegant if severely official structure, the Uffizi wraps like a horseshoe around its courtyard and stands between the Arno River and the Piazza della Signoria, or civic square. On the ground floor is an open portico with large carved doors leading to various offices. Above this portico rise two more stories, set off by projecting cornices, and finally what was once a roofed open gallery, a feature typical of ancient Florentine residences. From the beginning, the Medicis used this top floor for entertainment more than for bureaucratic functions. The airy gallery offers extraordinary views: to the south, the Arno and hills dominated by the Pitti Palace, the Fortezza del Belvedere, and the church of San Miniato al Monte; to the north, the piazza with views of the tower of the Palazzo Vecchio and the dome of Santa Maria del Fiore.

The idea of pairing Medici's superb art with these stunning views of nature and city life was stimulating and innovative, but it fell to another ruler and another architect to carry it out: Francesco (1541–1587), Cosimo's son, who assembled a refined collection; and Bernardo Buontalenti (1536–1608), a versatile Mannerist and a brilliant technician capable of giving shape to his patron's fantasies.

Their collaboration resulted in the nucleus of the future gallery in the great octagonal room called the Tribune and in the rooms off the east side of the palace's fourth floor. From 1590 the objects and works of art on display were listed in inventories, and these pages, together with early seventeenth-century descriptions and documentary images, such as the famous view of 1775 by Johann Zoffany (now in the English royal collections), offer a sense of the original appearance of these first museum rooms. The corridors were lined with ancient sculptures from the Roman period that still form one of the museum's most important collections.

The display included a variety of objects, in accordance with the eclectic taste popular at the time: not only paintings and sculpture, but also coins, medallions, small bronzes and pieces in precious stone, natural curiosities, scientific instruments, and weapons. Some rooms were dedicated to a single collection, and the ceilings of such rooms carried frescoes related to the objects on display.

Among the rooms, the Tribune was the museum's real jewel. (Sadly, its contemporary appearance offers only a glimpse of the dazzling splendor of its original arrangement, which was destroyed during the rule of the Lorraines in the eighteenth century.) The decoration of this room had a complex cosmological meaning: the design of the marble floors was an allusion to earth; the red fabric covering the walls alluded to fire; the octagonal vault was inlaid with mother-of-pearl and crowned by a wind rose, emblems of water and air. Medici symbols were scattered throughout the decoration, indicating that the ruling dynasty, responsible for the room's imposing collection of artistic and natural wonders, was prominent in the cosmic order. The walls were hung with paintings, and a shelf ran around the room at eye level bearing statuettes and small cases full of treasures. In the center of the room, like a miniature reproduction of the Tribune itself, stood an octagonal cabinet inlaid with precious stones; such inlay was typical of the grand ducal workshops, which were located in the west wing of the Uffizi. Over time, unique ancient sculptures from the Medici collection—including the *Venus de Medici,* the *Wrestlers,* and the *Knife-Grinder*—were added to the room and can still be seen there.

In the Tribune and adjacent rooms the Medici princes entertained illustrious allies and guests, ambassadors and sovereigns, showing off not only their refined taste but also the family's wealth and power. These rooms have since seen dramatic events tied to successive ruling dynasties followed by the unified Italian state and to changes in taste and in standards of display. Throughout this long process, the Medici acted as catalysts, for all the grand dukes saw the gallery as the pride of the family collections, and each labored to expand and embellish its rooms, which gradually took over the

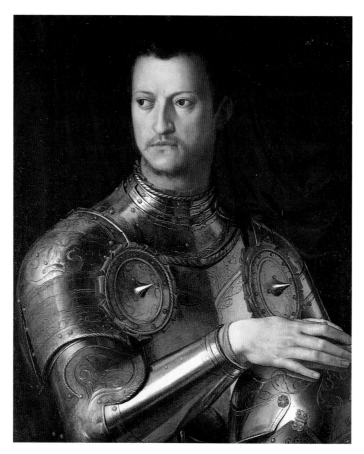

BRONZINO (1503–1572)
Cosimo I de' Medici, n.d.
Oil on wood, 27½ × 22¼ in. (71 × 57 cm)

entire fourth floor (except for a large area to the east, where Buontalenti had built a theater for Francesco). The collections grew to include miniatures, portraits, Etruscan relics, tapestries, ceramics, and bronzes; and the painting collection was constantly enlarged. The travels and intermarriages that linked the Medici to other courts of Italy and Europe greatly increased the family's opportunities for cultural exchange and enrichment. Even when the family's political position weakened, the descendants of Cosimo I were still able to procure the best European art through shrewd agents and far-flung connections, and they still had the wealth that permitted each family member—whether cardinal or duchess—to have his or her own court, palaces, villas, and favorite artists.

With foresight and generosity, the last Medici, Anna Maria Luisa (widow of the Elector Johann Wilhelm), drew up a family pact in 1737 binding the collections forever to the Uffizi and to Florence, thus avoiding the dispersion of a patrimony that had long since ceased to be "private" in any sense.

Subsequent acquisitions were made to update the collection or to include examples from periods or territories less well represented. These were only faint echoes of the splendors the Medici had amassed, for the family had followed the highest criteria and made sure choices in their purchases and commissions. Additions to the collection have been infrequent; recent ones include prestigious government acquisitions (two Goyas and an El Greco) and private donations that have filled out the antique self-portrait collection. (Also noteworthy are works that entered the museum with the Contini Bonacossi donation and the Siviero collection.)

The Lorraines, in keeping with the rationalism of the eighteenth century, reorganized the museum displays and reworked several rooms in a refined Neoclassical style, but they also removed collections not related to painting and ancient sculpture: some of these (weapons, silver) were dispersed, while other homogeneous groups went to form the bases of important Florentine museums, such as the Museum of Science and the Specola Museum of Natural History.

Thanks to the public character conferred on the Uffizi by the last Medici, the museum survived almost unscathed the confiscations of the Napoleonic period and the thefts of World War II. Today the Gallery displays ancient sculpture along the grand staircases and in the corridors and has forty-five rooms dedicated to painting from the thirteenth to the nineteenth century. These works are divided by school, according to the reorganization done after World War II. Other pieces are displayed in the Vasari Corridor, an area that is unfortunately not always open to the public. On the third floor of the building, in what was once the foyer of Francesco's now-destroyed theater, is the collection of drawings and prints. One of the most important of its kind in the world, the collection contains some 110,000 sheets. The building also houses the world's most important collection of self-portraits, started by Cardinal Leopoldo de' Medici and augmented in 1981, on the occasion of the 400th anniversary of the Uffizi, with a gift of 200 self-portraits donated by famous contemporary artists.

The paintings that appear in this book, and the other works currently on display, are of major importance; many pieces of comparable quality are in storage or are being temporarily held elsewhere. More than fifty paintings, and some statues, damaged by the bomb that exploded outside the walls of the Uffizi in May 1993 are to be restored; only three paintings, including Bartolomeo Manfredi's *Concert* (page 93) and Gerrit van Honthorst's *Adoration of the Shepherds*, were damaged beyond repair. Recent changes are promising: the two lower floors of the building, which had been occupied by the State Archives since approximately 1850, have been cleared, and the museum will soon expand throughout the building. This reorganization will involve not dramatic architectural changes, but rather a thorough restoration of the original Vasari rooms and redistribution of the displays to bring them into accordance with contemporary ideas about museum exhibition.

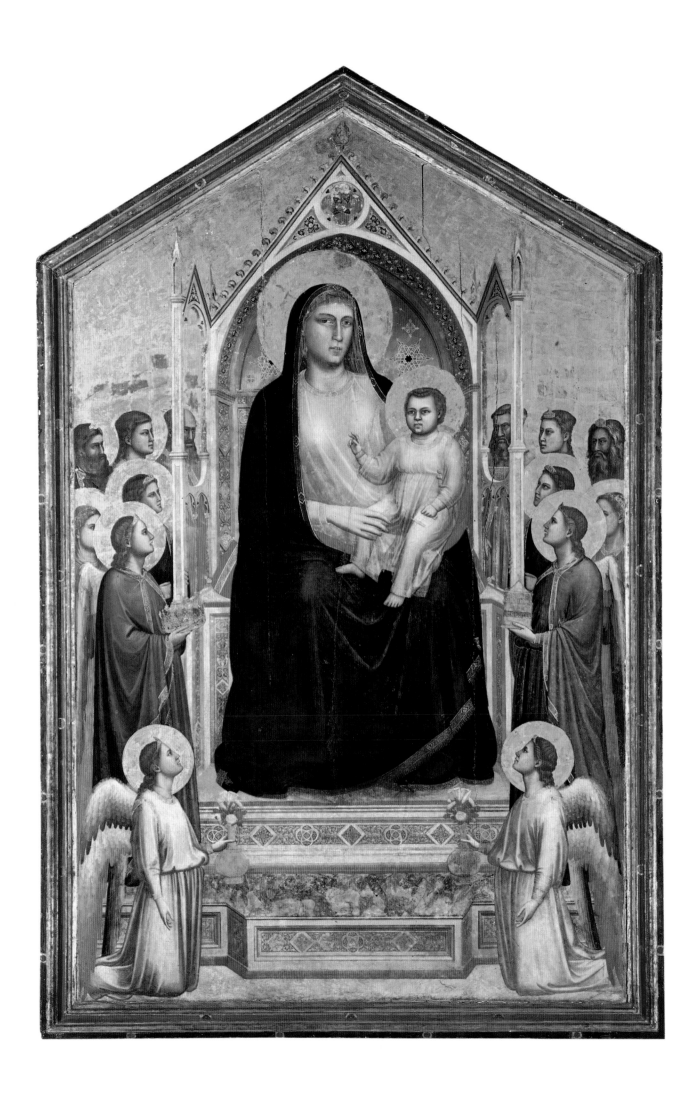

ITALIAN PAINTING

*T*HE OLDEST PAINTINGS ON DISPLAY in the Uffizi are Tuscan works of the thirteenth and four-teenth centuries. Some of these works still echo the Byzantine tradition; others show the early effects of the humanization of painting, which led artists to experiment with new techniques for examining and representing nature. Fundamental texts for subsequent Western art, the paintings of the Madonna and Child by Giovanni Cimabue, Duccio di Boninsegna, and Giotto (opposite) were all originally altarpieces in Florentine churches, where they offered divine images that were newly accessible because they were endowed with more recognizable human bodies and emotions.

Later generations, in both Florence and Siena, followed in the wake of these three leaders. In Simone Martini's famous *Annunciation,* the extraordinary use of gold and the gestures of the main characters create a courtly and aristocratic scene of humanity. The brothers Pietro and Am-brogio Lorenzetti were deeply influenced by the artistic environment of Florence; their different pictorial languages can be examined by comparing Ambrogio's *Presentation in the Temple* (page 18), which is so sumptuous and ornate that it recalls Byzantine art, with Pietro's *Scenes of the Life of the Blessed Umiltà* (page 17), which has a limited but clear palette and a poetically simple grandeur.

Representatives of the school of Giotto brought the master's teaching to the threshold of the fifteenth century. Among them was Giottino, who painted his elegiac *Pietà* presenting saints and humans sharing a silent sorrow; only the luminous colors ring out against the gold background. Of a slightly later date is Andrea Orcagna's majestic and dynamic *Saint Matthew* (page 21), whose folding triptych form recalls its original use on one of the pillars of the church of Orsanmichele.

An extraordinary artistic renewal spread from Florence at the beginning of the fifteenth cen-tury, and the seminal works from this period, which have made the Uffizi famous, express visu-ally the explosion of Renaissance concepts: the establishment of perspective derived from precise mathematical rules (rather than those intuited by Giotto); the rediscovery of classical antiquity; the search for the ideal relationships among figures and settings; and the new central position of man as protagonist in history and as the measure of all things. For example, Masaccio's render-ings of the the Madonna and Child (pages 26, 32) are at once classical and Christian in inspira-tion. When Paolo Uccello assembled his great scenes of the Battle of San Romano (in three parts: the other two are in the Louvre and the National Gallery of London; page 27), he took the nascent rules of perspective to the limit, rendering the epic battle scene unreal and bloodless, with merry-go-round horses and suits of armor, all arranged stiffly within chessboard grids dra-matically marked off by pikes, crossbows, and broken lances on the ground.

Among the fundamental advances of this period is the natural luminosity that infuses the col-ors in the *Magnoli Altarpiece* by Domenico Veneziano (page 28). The artist's stay in Florence was of great importance both to the local painting school and to Piero della Francesca, who worked side by side with Domenico on the frescoes of Saint Egidio (now lost). The paired portraits of the Duke and Duchess of Urbino (page 30) are among the best-known works by Piero della Francesca; by the time he painted these he had already perfected his synthesis of perspective and luminosity.

OPPOSITE: GIOTTO (C. 1266–C. 1337)
Madonna in Glory, 1310
Tempera on wood, 126¾ × 79½ in. (325 × 204 cm)

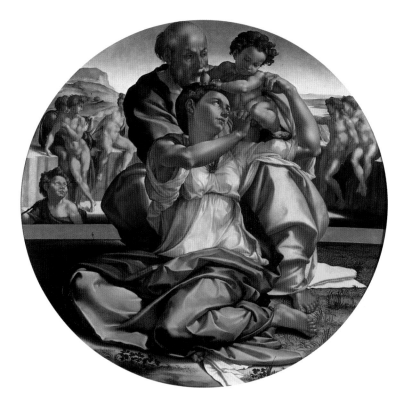

MICHELANGELO BUONARROTI (1475–1564)
The Holy Family (The Doni Tondo), 1504
Tempera on wood, diameter: 47¼ in. (120 cm)

Fra Filippo Lippi proved himself a restless experimenter, inventing influential prototypes for Florentine art such as the famous *Madonna and Child with Two Angels* (page 29), the first profane interpretation of a religious subject. Other artists made even more daring experiments, particularly Antonio Pollaiolo, who probed the dynamics of figure relationships and space, as in the small tablet depicting one of the "Labors of Hercules" (page 36).

The Neoplatonic school assembled around the Medici brought ancient myths into fashion; Sandro Botticelli took these and made their symbolic and philosophical meanings his own. The Uffizi possesses the world's most important collection of these works, including his *Primavera* (page 42) and *The Birth of Venus* (page 43). The fluid lines of his drawing and the aristocratic grace and melancholy of his figures reflect a bright moment of faith in humanistic ideals. But that moment passed, and near the end of the century Botticelli turned to a devout reworking of the most traditional religious motifs, as seen in the grandiose and radiant *Coronation of the Virgin* (page 44), only recently put back on display after a long restoration.

The Uffizi collection includes other works that introduced dramatic changes to Italian painting: works by Leonardo da Vinci, with their "scientific"—rather than idealized and symbolic—vision of nature. They include the *Baptism of Christ* (page 50), on which Leonardo worked alongside Verrocchio—whose workshop was the training ground for many talents at the end of the fifteenth century—and Leonardo's youthful *Annunciation* (page 49), with its traditional composition refreshed by the sfumato technique and by the painter's atmospheric filter, as well as his highly complex and revolutionary *Adoration of the Magi* (page 51).

Michelangelo transmitted a sculptural, sophisticated, and intellectual vision in his *Holy Family* (also known as the *Doni Tondo;* above). Recent restoration of this work shows the iridescent and strident colors borrowed by the first generations of Mannerist painters, who looked to Michelangelo as their master. This splendid work, almost the only panel by Michelangelo, presents the holy family in a perfectly fused design, with the foreground figures contrasted by monochrome nudes in the background. Another tutelary artist of fundamental importance to

Italian painting was Raphael. In the Uffizi are his moving *Madonna del Cardellino* (page 61) and the portrait of Pope Leo X (page 5), with its powerful colors and psychological insight.

The works of the Mannerists—Jacopo da Pontormo, Rosso Fiorentino, and the Sienese Domenico Beccafumi—mark the movement away from objective naturalism toward an intellectual style that is by turns deeply moving, mocking, or ironic. They feature an extension of shapes, the use of unnatural colors, the influence of prints from northern Europe, and the disruption of the equilibrium of fifteenth-century painting. Later in the sixteenth century Florentine Mannerists moved toward the precious and formal, as in the cold, courtly works by Bronzino, the ideal court portraitist, who was trusted by the Medici to present them in timeless, regal images. Florentine Mannerists then turned to the production of small, sophisticated paintings based on allegorical or mythological subjects.

Andrea Mantegna's *Portrait of a Cardinal* (page 34) is of particular interest, for recent restoration has revealed the brightness of its colors and the sculptural sense of the sharply defined face. Another masterpiece is his triptych with *The Adoration of the Magi* in the center flanked by *The Ascension* and *The Circumcision* (page 34), where each of the three subjects has a different setting.

In contrast to these are the balanced and harmonious compositions of Perugino, which all share an unforced elegance and simplicity. The power of his pictorial style is particularly evident in the *Pietà* (page 45), in which large arches set off the scene in a classical tableau of grief. Also in the collection are the powerful panels by Luca Signorelli, including the tondo of the Holy Family (page 46), crammed with intersecting views of bodies and books.

Correggio, whose mellow paintings are permeated with tenderness, as in the languid *Adoration of the Child* (page 68), was a point of reference in the sixteenth century, and he influenced artists beyond the local school. Beyond Tuscany, other fifteenth-century Italian schools of painting are well represented in the Uffizi, including pieces of fundamental importance from the Veneto region. The works by Giovanni Bellini, for example, include the mysterious *Sacred Allegory* and the monochrome *Lamentation over the Body of Christ* (page 33) as well as the grandiose *Saint Jerome.* At the end of the century, and well into the sixteenth century, the dominant artist in the Veneto was Titian, who throughout his long life was ever attentive to changes in the artistic climate. His masterpieces hang side by side in the Uffizi, including the *Venus of Urbino* (page 67), which entered the Medici collection in 1631 with the marriage of Vittoria della Rovere to Ferdinando II. That work offers an expression of full Renaissance opulence; Titian later showed his awareness of the Mannerist style with his *Venus and Cupid.* The collection also includes works by Titian's successors, such as the luminous and expansive paintings of Paolo Veronese and the shadowy, visionary works of Tintoretto.

Parmigianino's works display a certain softness based on the influence of Correggio as well as his virtuosity as a colorist, his elegantly elongated figures, and the ambiguity in their faces. Dosso Dossi of Ferrara (like Parmigianino, from the region of Emilia) was of a somewhat tougher temper and used brighter colors as well as unsettling symbolism, as in *Witchcraft* (page 68).

The more exaggerated and Baroque aspects of Mannerism gave way to the styles of Caravaggio and of Annibale Carracci later in the sixteenth century. Caravaggio took the tradition of Lombard realism to new heights with his dramatic use of lighting and sense of proximity to the scene. In his *Young Bacchus* (page 90), the mythological character is presented without disguise, in a rendering that has the lucid brilliance of a still life. The same detachment from myth can be seen in the vigorous and deeply felt *Sacrifice of Isaac* (page 88), with its peasant brutality, and in the *Medusa* (page 89), which abandons the sterility of the ancient symbol to confront the viewer with the startling image of a bloody severed head. In comparison to these works is the great *Venus with Satyr and Cupids* (page 88) by Annibale Carracci, which demonstrates a more conventional technique, but with rich impasto and expanded forms, and a closer adhesion to classical myth.

Little else from the seventeenth century in Italy is on view in the main galleries, for most of the works of that period are displayed in the long Vasari Corridor or are still in storage awaiting the expansion of the Uffizi. Even so, there is a broad selection of works by painters from throughout the peninsula, including the formidable Artemisia Gentileschi, whose fame as an artist and as a woman has been revived by recent exhibitions and publications. The Uffizi presents, among other works, her celebrated *Judith and Holofernes* (page 94), once the emblem of international feminism.

The Italian eighteenth century appears with such brilliant personalities as Giuseppe Maria Crespi from Bologna and Alessandro Magnasco of Genoa. Magnasco's gloomy or stormy scenes are peopled by priests and gypsies rendered with caustic humor; Crespi was an affectionate observer of the everyday life of common people. Grand Prince Ferdinando de' Medici was quickly won over by the immediacy and liveliness of Crespi's works, and almost all the paintings by Crespi in the Uffizi were made for him, including *The Painter's Family* and *The Flea* (page 102).

Above all, however, it is the Veneto school that represents the pictorial aspects of the Age of Enlightenment. Pietro Longhi in *The Confession* (a subject that would have been dear to Crespi; page 107) observes contemporary society without the bitter irony of his contemporary, William Hogarth. In contrast with Longhi's more traditional and often more robust characters are masterful works in pastel by the great portraitist Rosalba Carriera (the portrait of Felicità Sartori, page 103, is an example), known for the attractive faces of her women and female allegorical figures.

With technical virtuosity and colors drenched in light, Giovanni Battista Tiepolo created masterpieces of the great tradition of grandiloquent paintings that decorated ceilings (which explains why the view is from below, looking up) with his *Erection of a Statue to an Emperor* (page 105). The rational and scientific side of the century is more evident in Canaletto's famous views of Venice (*The Ducal Palace and Piazza San Marco;* below), in which the landscape, although rendered with faithful clarity, takes on an elegiac air thanks to the subdued colors and the theatrical composition.

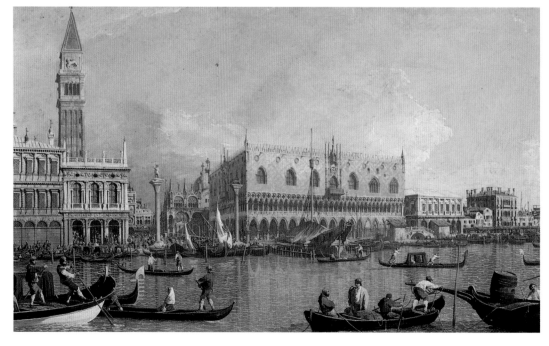

CANALETTO (1697–1768)
The Ducal Palace and Piazza San Marco, before 1755
Oil on canvas, 20 × 32 in. (51 × 83 cm)

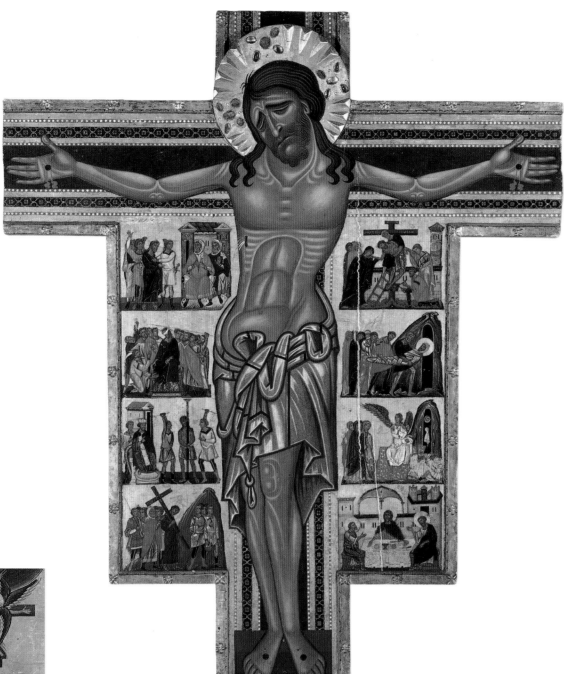

MASTER OF THE SAN FRANCESCO BARDI (active 1240–1270)
Crucifix with Stories of the Passion, n.d.
Tempera on wood, 97½ × 78 in. (250 × 200 cm)

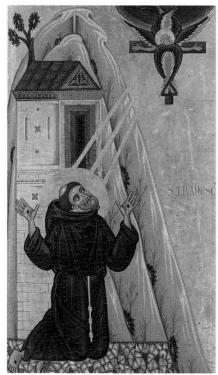

MASTER OF THE SAN FRANCESCO
BARDI (active 1240–1270)
Saint Francis Receiving the Stigmata, c. 1250
Tempera on wood, 31½ × 20 in. (81 × 51 cm)

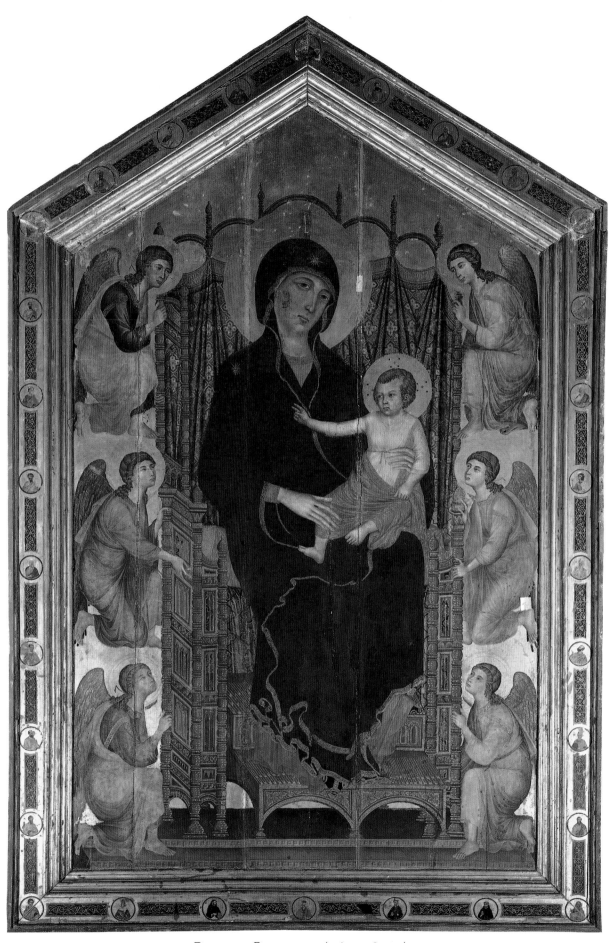

DUCCIO DI BONINSEGNA (active 1278–1319)
Maestà (Rucellai Madonna), 1285
Tempera on wood, 14 ft. 7½ in. × 9 ft. 5 in. (4.50 × 2.90 m)

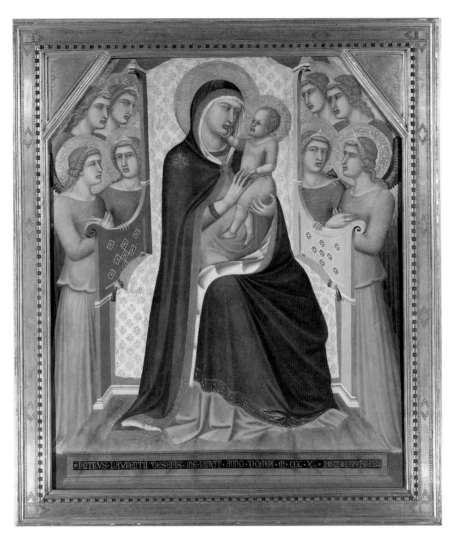

PIETRO LORENZETTI (C. 1280–C. 1348)
Madonna Enthroned with Angels, early 1340s
Tempera on wood, 56½ × 47½ in. (145 × 122 cm)

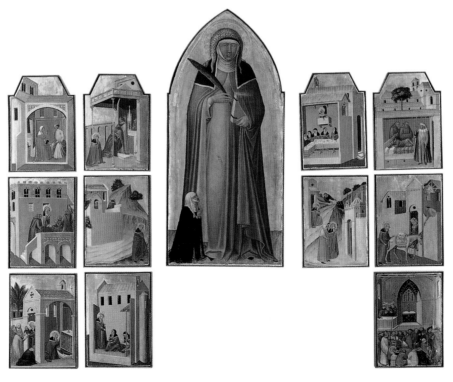

PIETRO LORENZETTI (C. 1280–C. 1348)
Scenes of the Life of the Blessed Umiltà, c. 1340
Tempera on wood, 50 × 22 in. (128 × 57 cm)

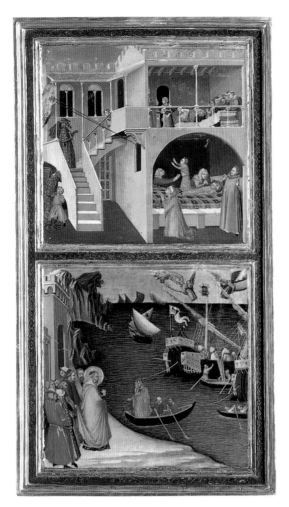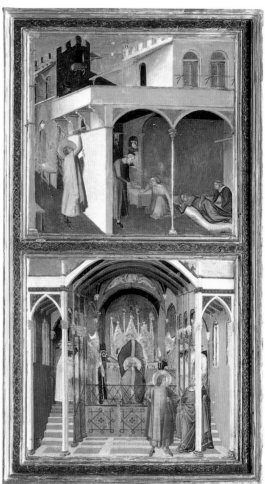

AMBROGIO LORENZETTI (1285–1348)
Scenes from the Life of Saint Nicholas, 1330
Tempera on wood, each panel: 37½ × 13½ in. (96 × 35 cm)

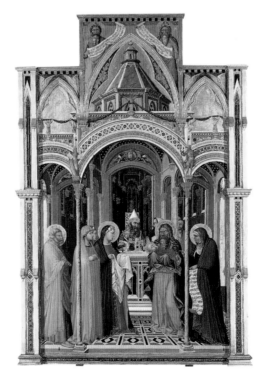

AMBROGIO LORENZETTI (1285–1348)
The Presentation in the Temple, 1342
Tempera on wood, 100 × 65½ in. (257 × 168 cm)

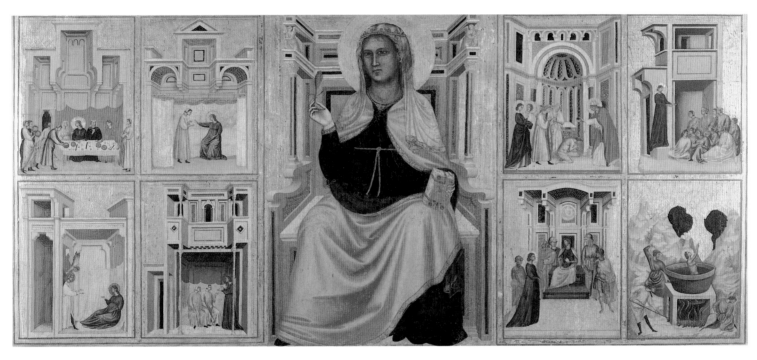

MASTER OF SAINT CECILIA (active c. 1300–1320)
Scenes from the Life of Saint Cecilia, after 1304
Tempera on wood, 33 × 71¼ in. (85 × 181 cm)

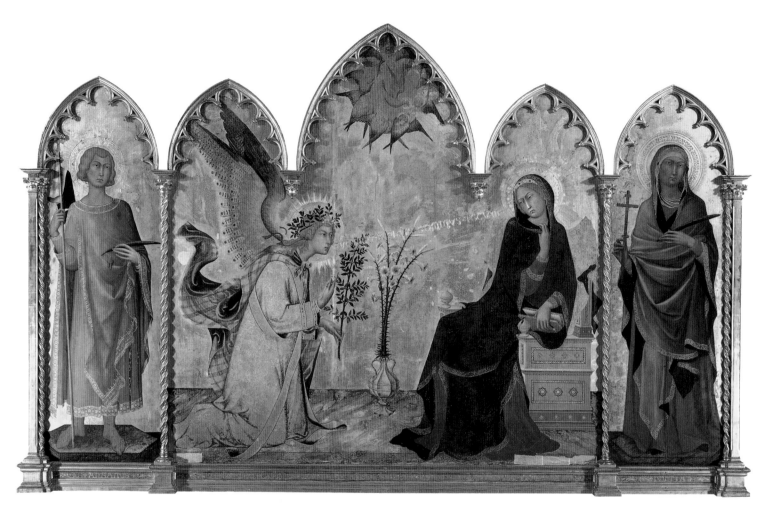

SIMONE MARTINI (C. 1283–1344)
and LIPPO MEMMI (active in Siena 1317–1347)
The Annunciation and Two Saints, 1333
Tempera on wood, 71¾ × 82 in. (184 × 210 cm)

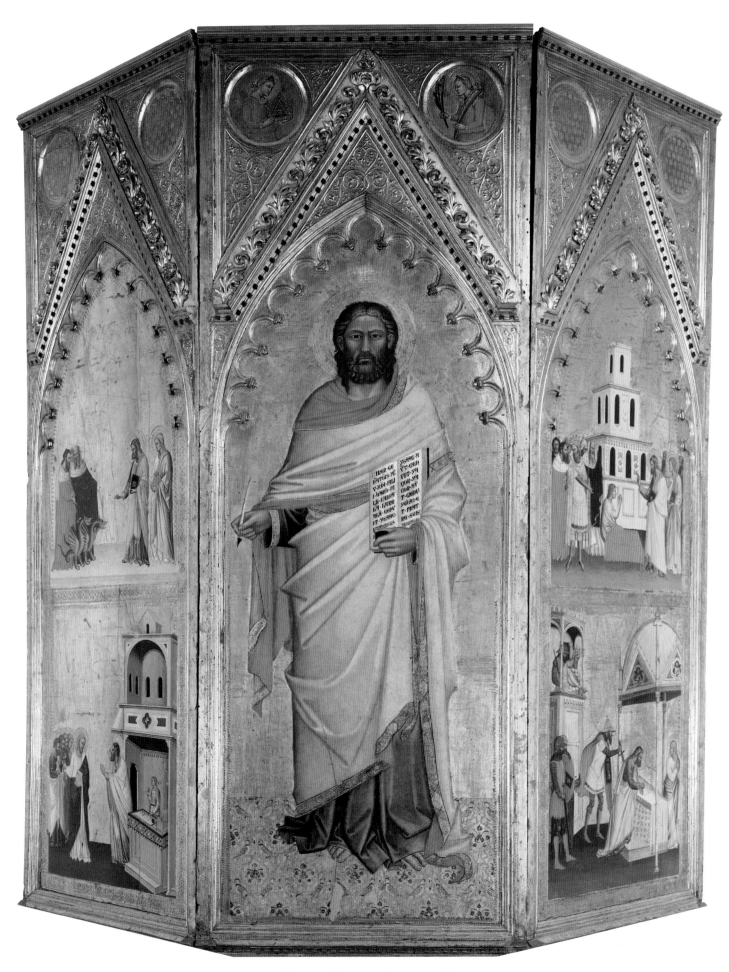

Andrea Orcagna (c. 1320–1368)
and Jacopo di Cione (c. 1330–1398)
Saint Matthew and Stories of His Life, c. 1367–70
Tempera on wood, 113½ × 103 in. (291 × 265 cm) overall

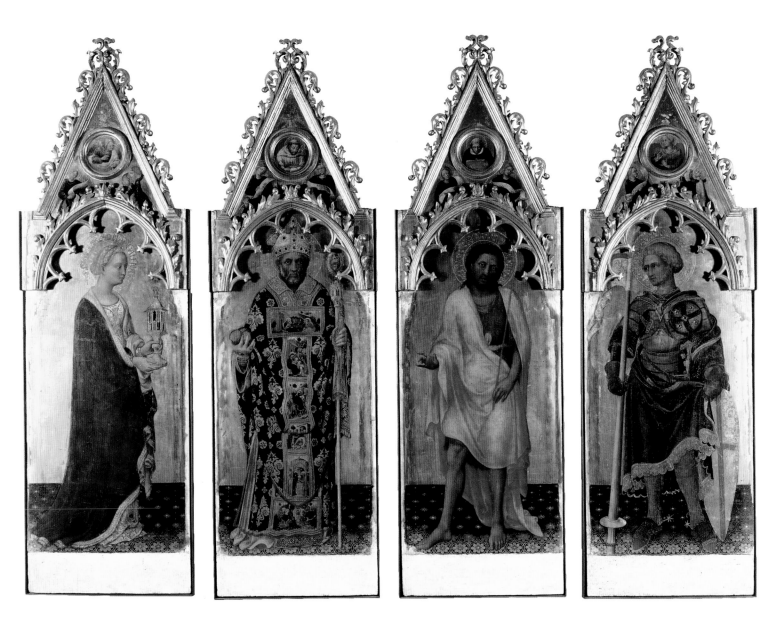

GENTILE DA FABRIANO (c. 1370–1427)
Four Saints of the Quaratesi Polyptych, 1425
Tempera on wood, each panel: 78 × 23½ in. (200 × 60 cm)

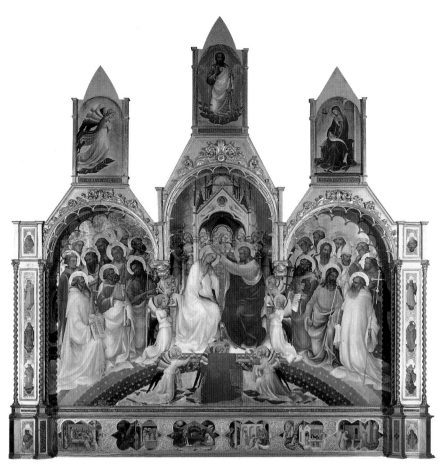

LORENZO MONACO (c. 1370–1425?)
The Coronation of the Virgin, 1413
Tempera on wood, 14 ft. 7½ in. × 11 ft. 4½ in. (4.50 × 3.50 m)

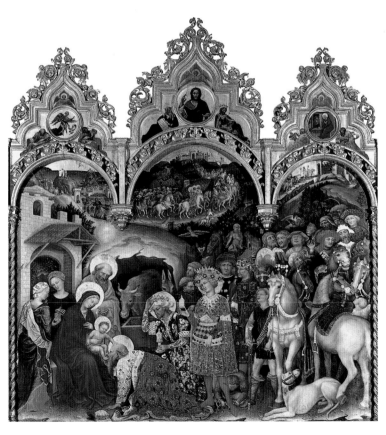

GENTILE DA FABRIANO (c. 1370–1427)
The Adoration of the Magi, 1423
Tempera on wood, 117 × 111 in. (300 × 283 cm)

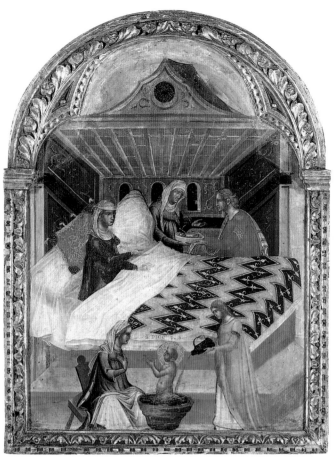

PAOLO VENEZIANO (active c. 1333–1362)
The Birth of Saint Nicholas, c. 1346
Tempera on wood, 29 × 21 in. (74.5 × 54.5 cm)

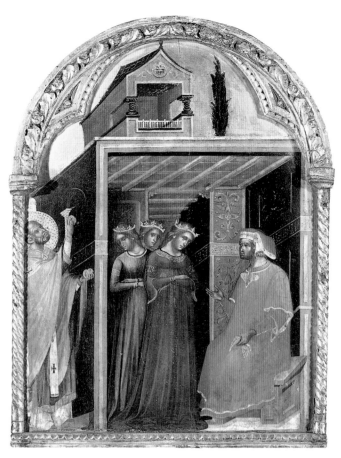

PAOLO VENEZIANO (active c. 1333–1362)
The Charity of Saint Nicholas, c. 1346
Tempera on wood, 28½ × 20½ in. (73 × 53 cm)

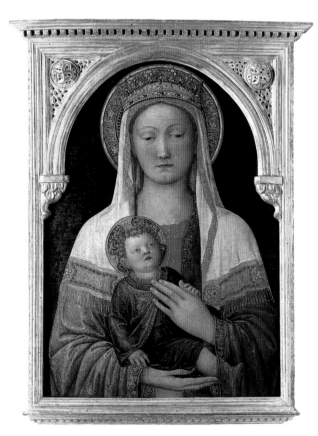

JACOPO BELLINI (c. 1400–1470)
Madonna and Child, c. 1450
Tempera on wood, 28½ × 22 in. (73 × 57 cm)

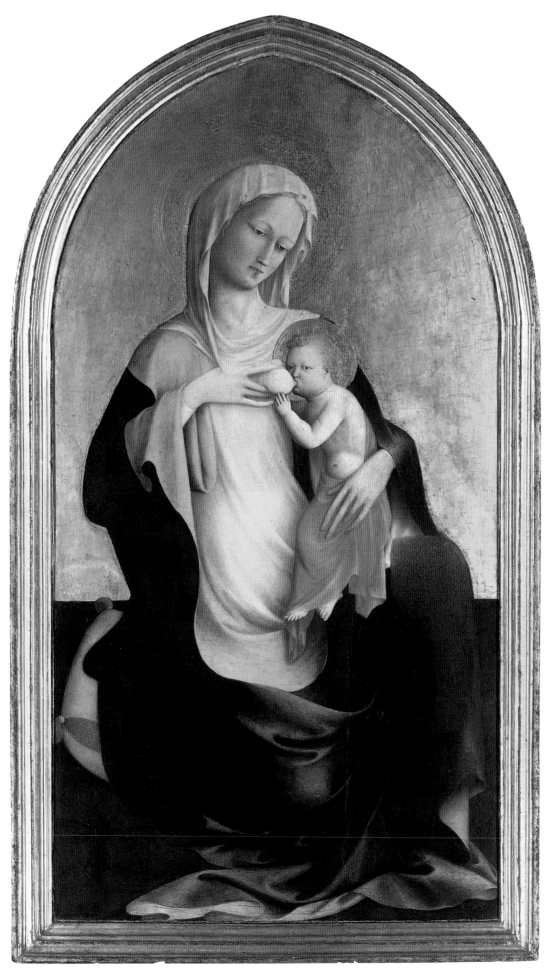

MASOLINO DA PANICALE (1383–c. 1447)
Madonna of Humility, 1430–35
Tempera on wood, 43 × 24 in. (110.5 × 62 cm)

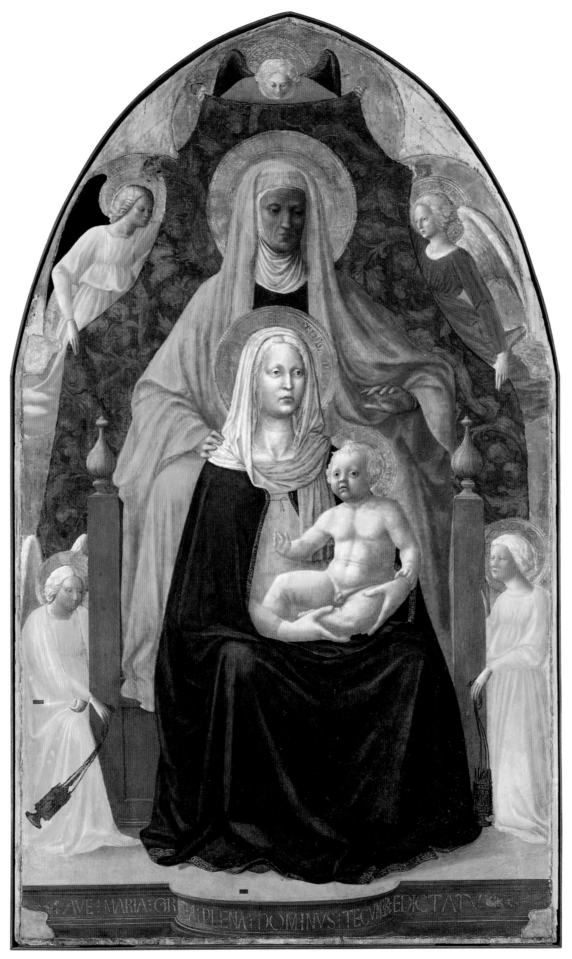

MASOLINO DA PANICALE (1383–c. 1447)
and MASACCIO (1401–1428?)
Madonna and Child with Saint Anne, 1424–25
Tempera on wood, 68¼ × 40 in. (175 × 103 cm)

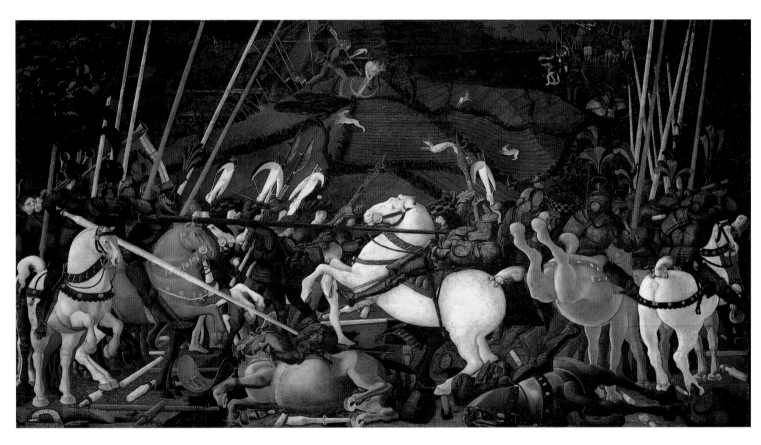

PAOLO UCCELLO (1397–1475)
The Battle of San Romano, c. 1456
Tempera on wood, 71 × 86 in. (182 × 220 cm)

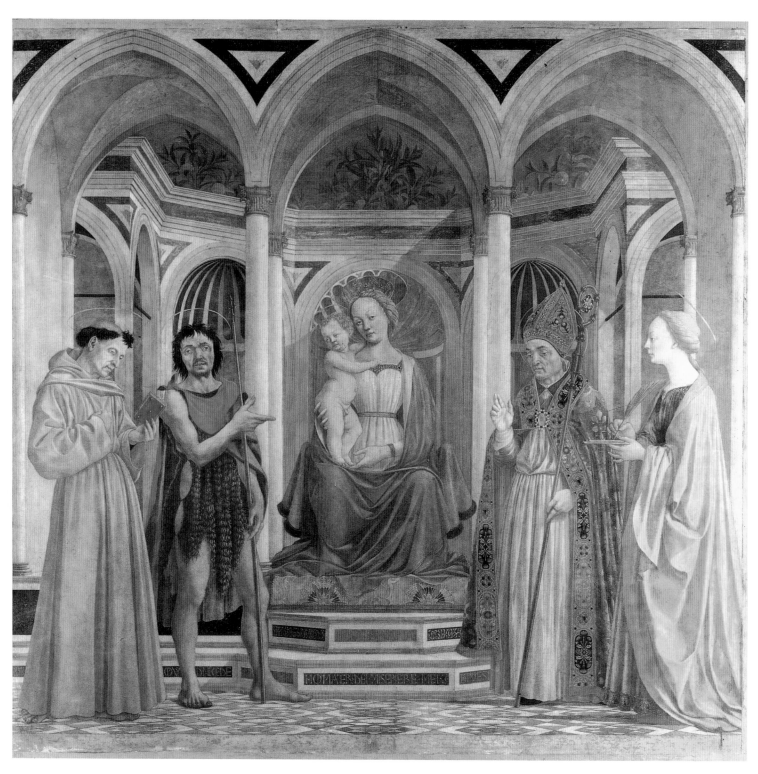

DOMENICO VENEZIANO (c. 1400–1461)
Madonna and Child with Saints (Magnoli Altarpiece), 1440–50
Tempera on wood, 81½ × 84¼ in. (209 × 216 cm)

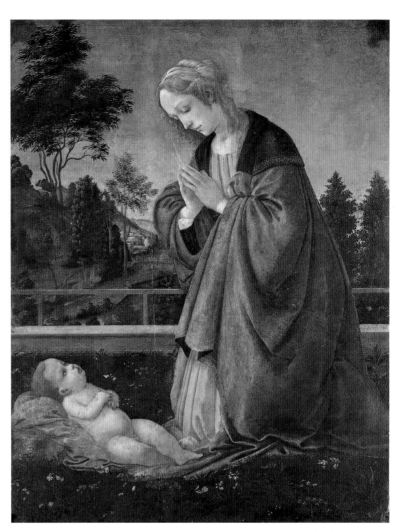

FILIPPINO LIPPI (c. 1457–1504)
The Adoration of the Child, early 1480s
Oil on wood, 37½ × 27½ in. (96 × 71 cm)

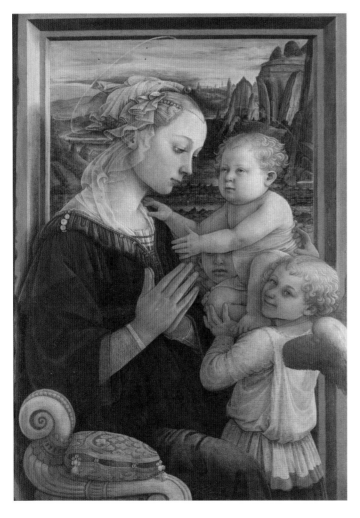

FRA FILIPPO LIPPI (c. 1406–1469)
Madonna and Child with Two Angels, c. 1464
Tempera on wood, 37 × 24 in. (95 × 62 cm)

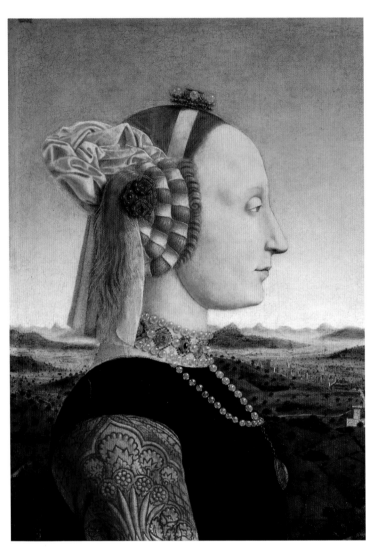

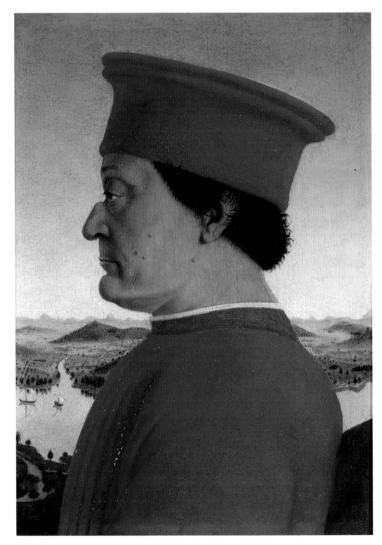

PIERO DELLA FRANCESCA (c. 1420–1492)
The Duchess of Urbino, 1465–70
Tempera on wood, 18 × 13 in. (47 × 33 cm)

PIERO DELLA FRANCESCA (c. 1420–1492)
The Duke of Urbino, 1465–70
Tempera on wood, 18 × 13 in. (47 × 33 cm)

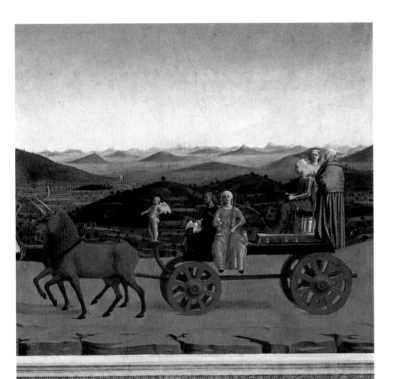

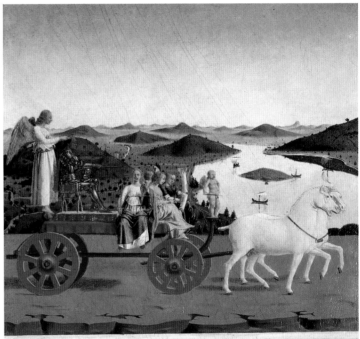

PIERO DELLA FRANCESCA (c. 1420–1492)
The Duchess of Urbino (verso), 1465–70
Tempera on wood, 18 × 13 in. (47 × 33 cm)

PIERO DELLA FRANCESCA (c. 1420–1492)
The Duke of Urbino (verso), 1465–70
Tempera on wood, 18 × 13 in. (47 × 33 cm)

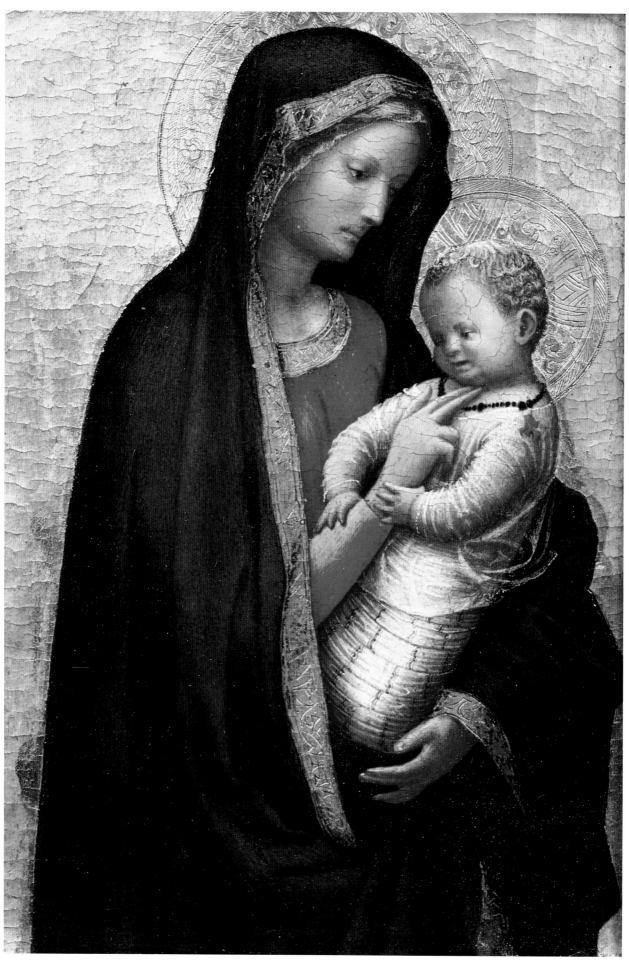

MASACCIO (1401–1428?)
Madonna and Child, c. 1426
Tempera on wood, 9½ × 7 in. (24.5 × 18.2 cm)

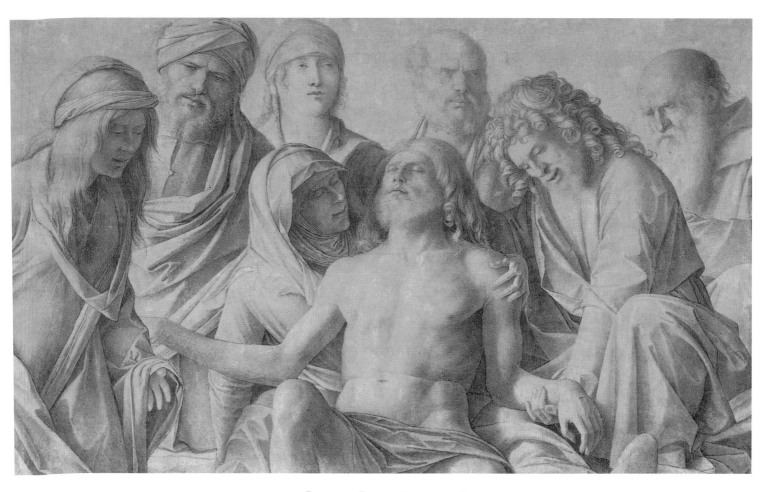

GIOVANNI BELLINI (c. 1430–1516)
The Lamentation over the Body of Christ, c. 1500
Tempera on wood, 29 × 46 in. (74 × 118 cm)

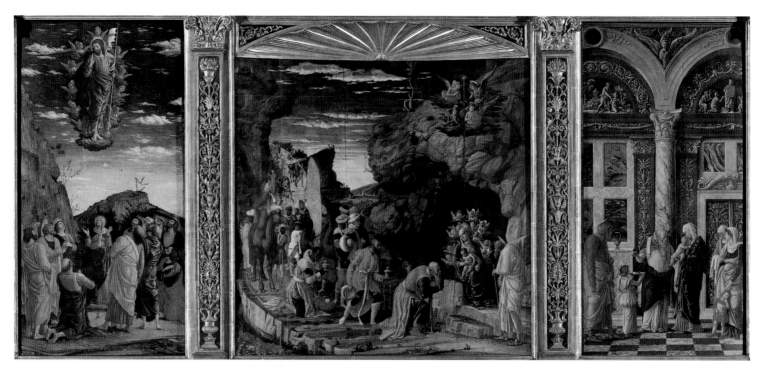

ANDREA MANTEGNA (1431–1506)
The Ascension, The Adoration of the Magi, and The Circumcision, 1463/67
Tempera on wood, 34 × 63⅝ in. (86.5 × 161.5 cm) overall

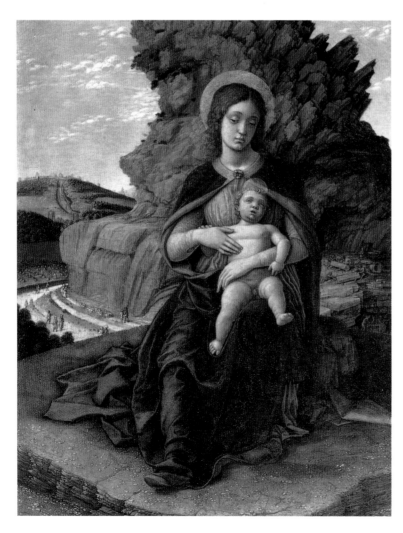

ANDREA MANTEGNA (1431–1506)
Madonna and Child, c. 1506
Tempera on wood, 11 × 8¼ in. (29 × 21.5 cm)

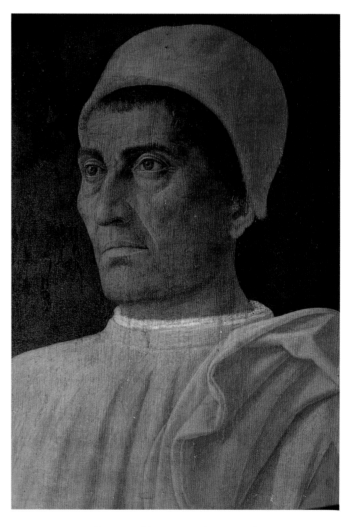

ANDREA MANTEGNA (1431–1506)
Portrait of a Cardinal, 1459/66
Tempera on wood, 16 × 11½ in. (40.4 × 29.5 cm)

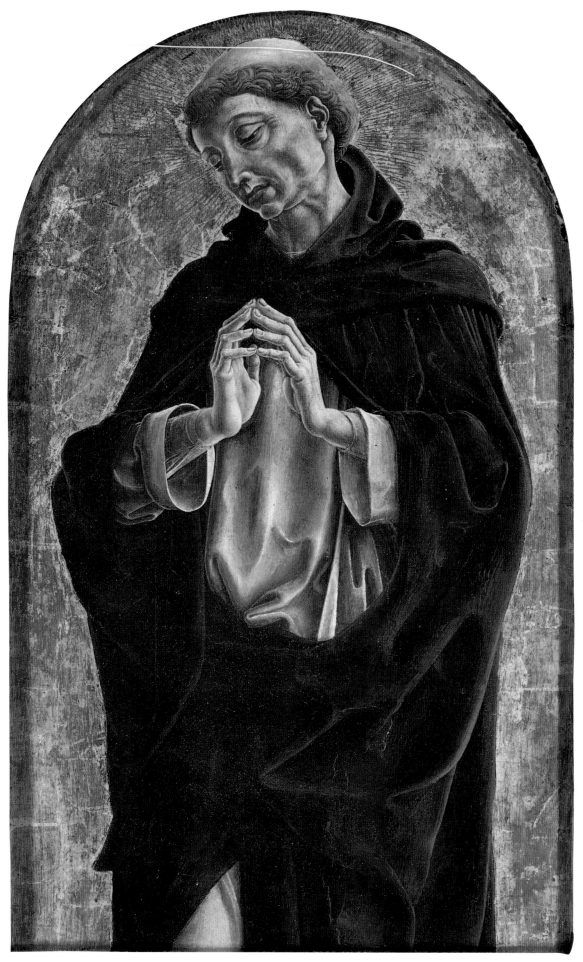

COSMÉ TURA (1432–1495)
Saint Dominic, c. 1475
Tempera on wood, 20 × 12½ in. (51 × 32 cm)

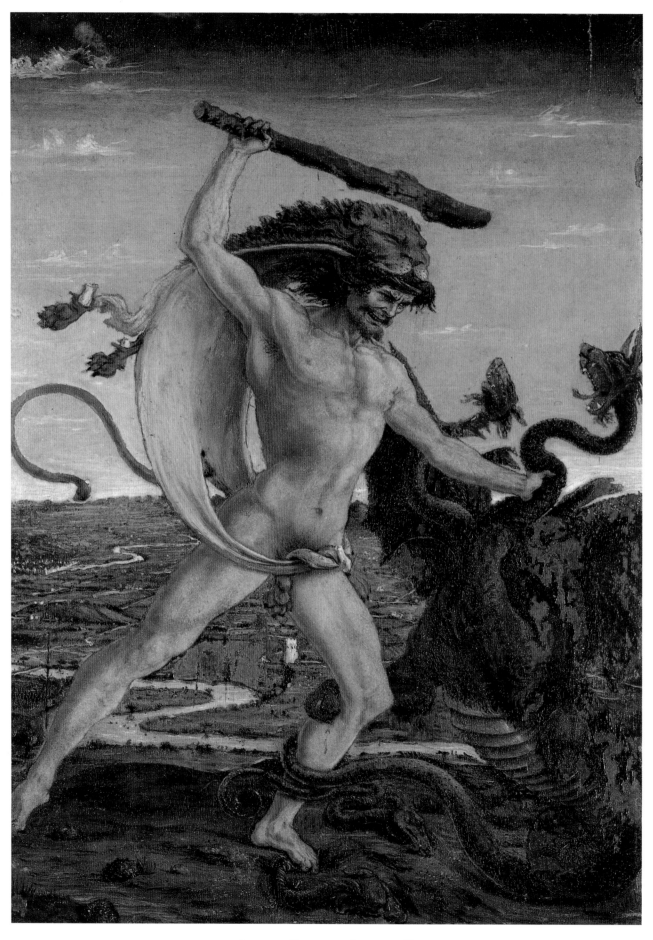

ANTONIO POLLAIOLO (c. 1431–1498)
Hercules and the Hydra, c. 1460
Tempera on wood, 6 ¾ × 4 ½ in. (17 × 12 cm)

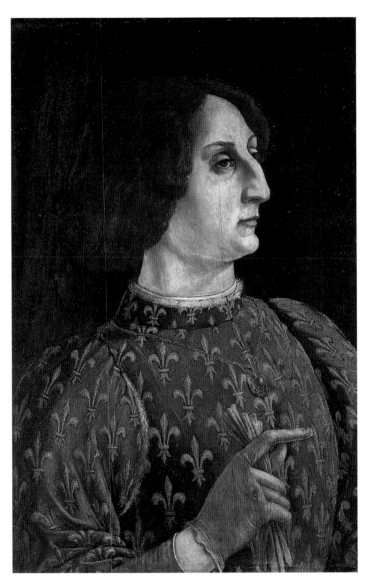

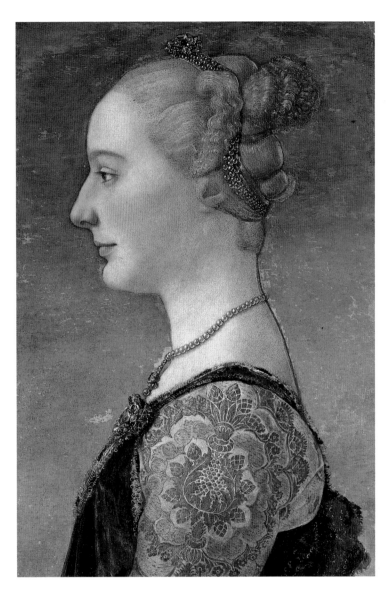

PIERO POLLAIOLO (1443–1496)
Galeazzo Maria Sforza, 1471
Tempera on wood, 25 × 16 in. (65 × 42 cm)

ANTONIO POLLAIOLO (c. 1431–1498)
Portrait of a Young Woman, c. 1475
Tempera on wood, 21½ × 13¾ in. (55 × 34 cm)

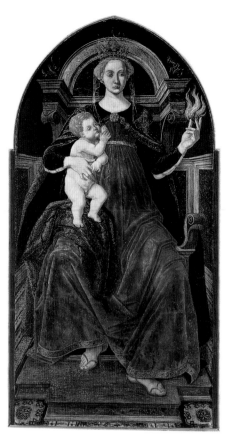

PIERO POLLAIOLO (1443–1496)
Charity, 1469
Tempera on wood, 65 × 34 in. (167 × 88 cm)

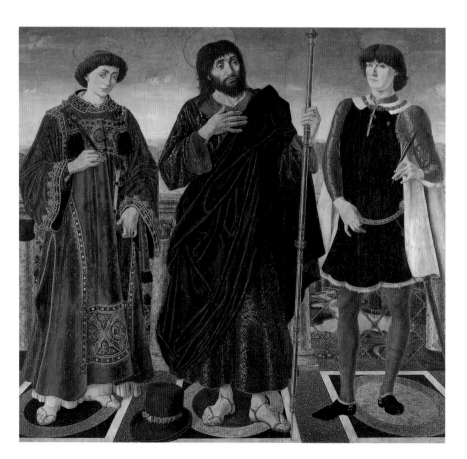

ANTONIO POLLAIOLO (c. 1431–1498)
and PIERO POLLAIOLO (1443–1496)
Saints Vincent, James, and Eustace, c. 1467
Tempera on wood, 67 × 70 in. (172 × 179 cm)

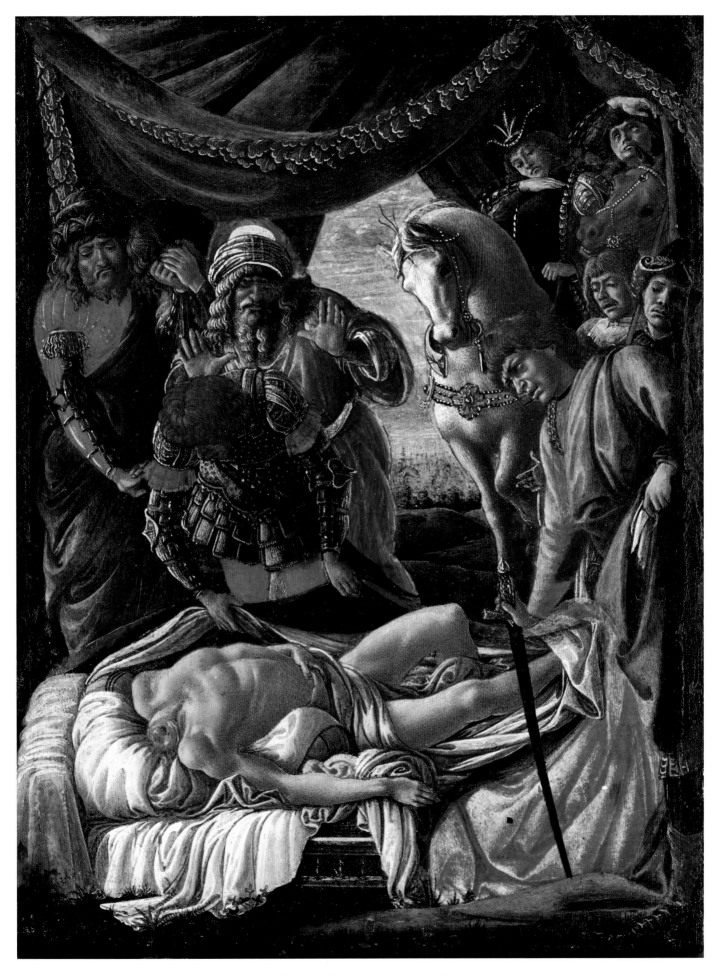

SANDRO BOTTICELLI (1445–1510)
Discovery of the Body of Holofernes, before 1480
Tempera on wood, 12 × 9¾ in. (31 × 25 cm)

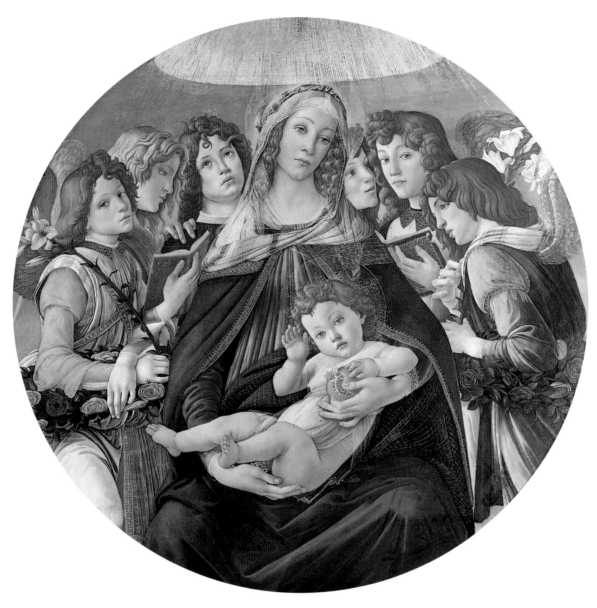

SANDRO BOTTICELLI (1445–1510)
Madonna of the Pomegranate, before 1490
Tempera on wood, diameter: 56 in. (143.5 cm)

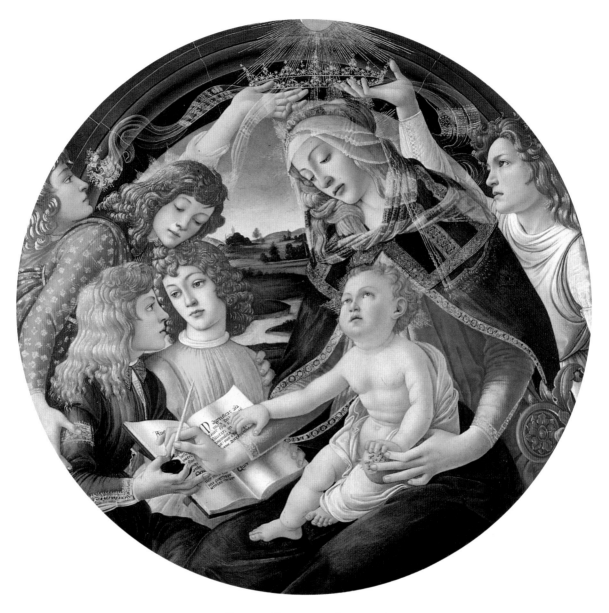

SANDRO BOTTICELLI (1445–1510)
Madonna of the Magnificat, before 1490
Tempera on wood, diameter: 46 in. (118 cm)

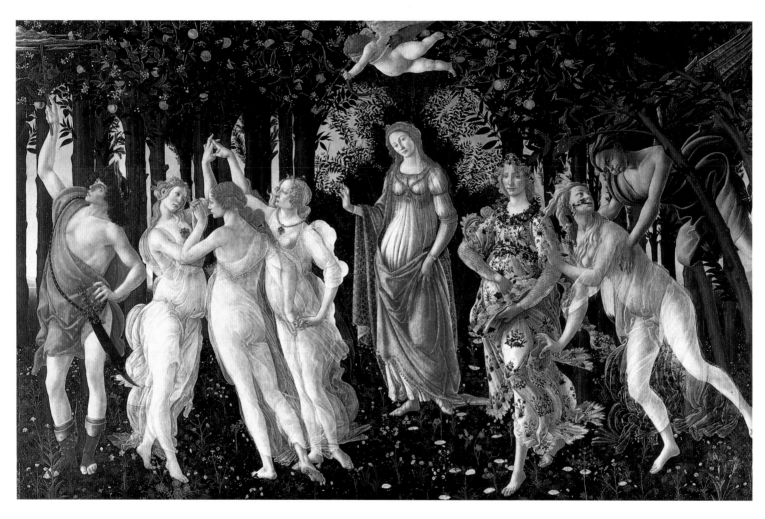

SANDRO BOTTICELLI (1445–1510)
Primavera, 1477–80
Tempera on wood, 79⅞ × 123⅝ in. (203 × 314 cm)

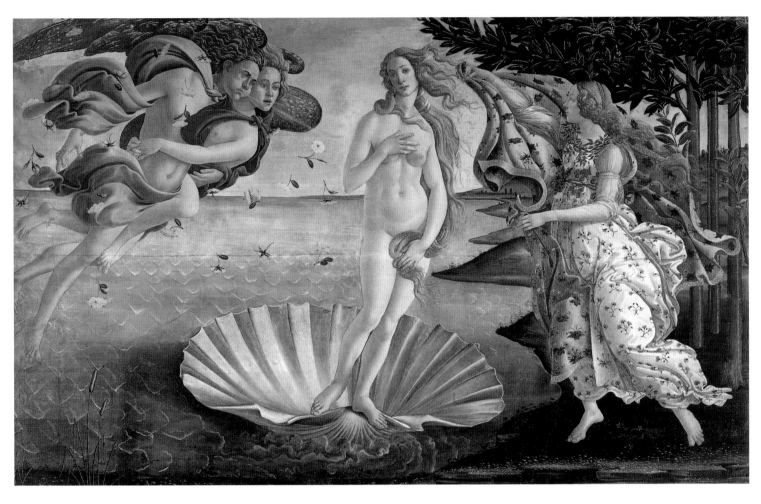

SANDRO BOTTICELLI (1445–1510)
The Birth of Venus, c. 1480
Tempera on canvas, 67¼ × 108 in. (172.5 × 278.5 cm)

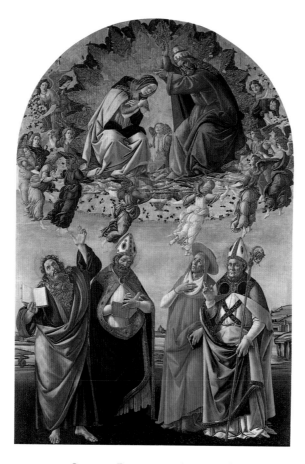

SANDRO BOTTICELLI (1445–1510)
The Coronation of the Virgin, c. 1489
Tempera on wood, 12 ft. 3½ in. × 8 ft. 5⅝ in. (3.78 × 25.8 m)

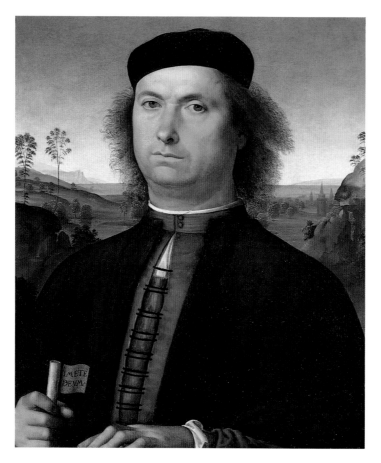

PERUGINO (c. 1445–1523)
Francesco delle Opere, 1494
Tempera on wood, 20 × 17 in. (52 × 44 cm)

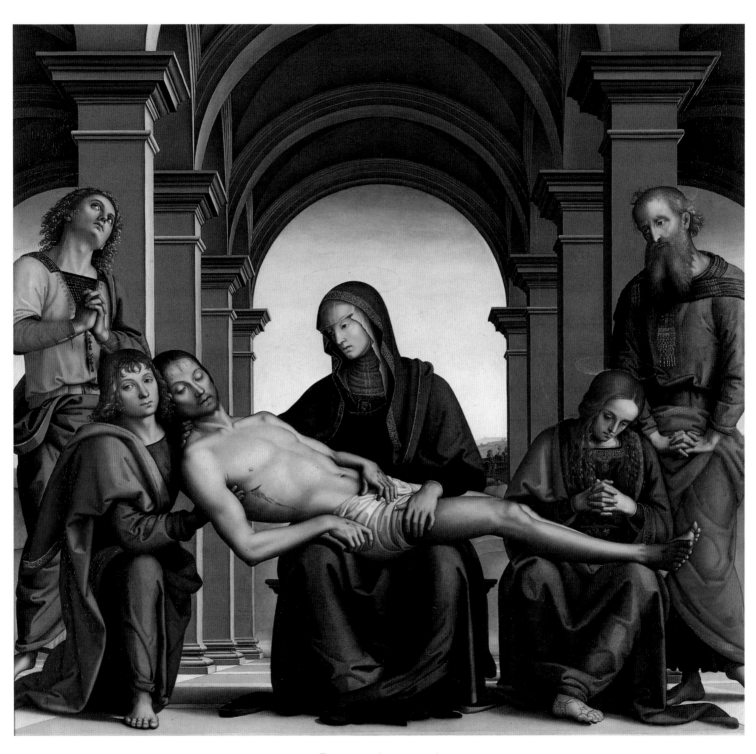

PERUGINO (c. 1445–1523)
Pietà, 1493/94
Tempera on wood, 65½ × 68½ in. (168 × 176 cm)

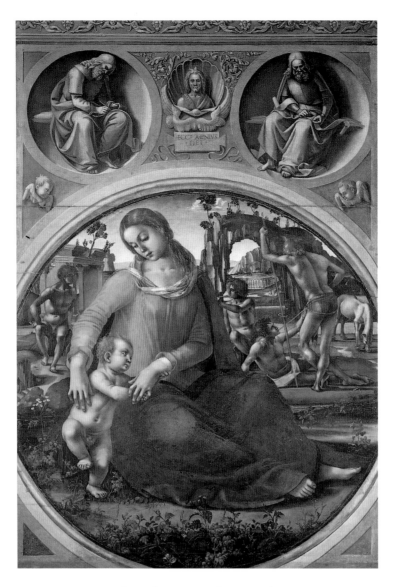

LUCA SIGNORELLI (1441?–1523)
Madonna and Child, 1490–95
Oil on wood, 66 × 46 in. (170 × 117.5 cm)

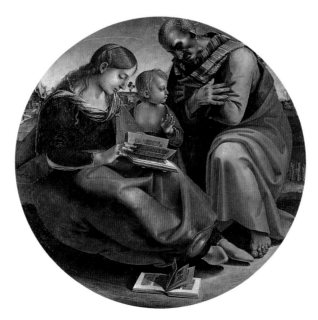

LUCA SIGNORELLI (1441?–1523)
The Holy Family, c. 1490
Oil on wood, diameter: 48 in. (124 cm)

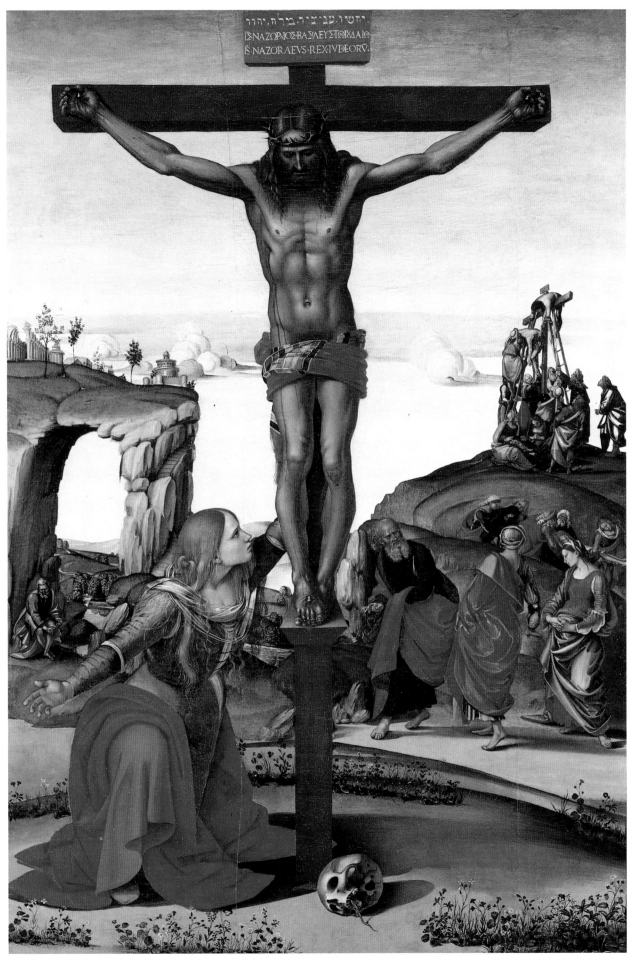

LUCA SIGNORELLI (1441?–1523)
The Crucifixion with Mary Magdalene, c. 1500
Oil on canvas, 96 × 64 in. (247 × 165 cm)

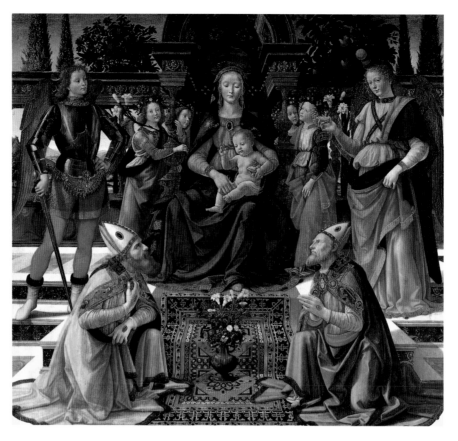

DOMENICO GHIRLANDAIO (1449–1494)
Madonna Enthroned with Saints, c. 1484
Tempera on wood, 74 × 78 in. (190 × 200 cm)

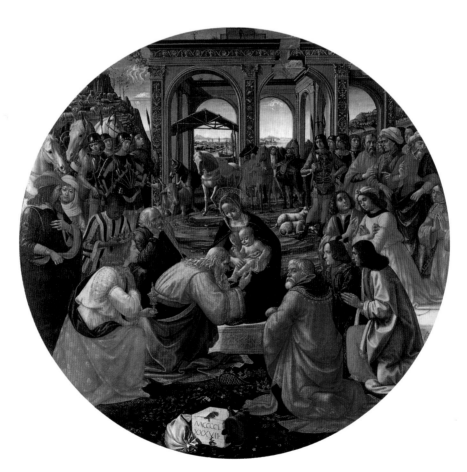

DOMENICO GHIRLANDAIO (1449–1494)
The Adoration of the Magi, 1487
Tempera on wood, diameter: 67 in. (172 cm)

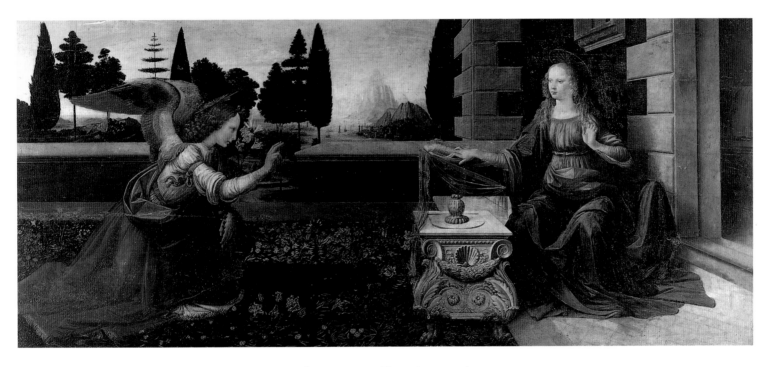

LEONARDO DA VINCI (1452–1519)
The Annunciation, c. 1472–75
Oil on wood, 34⅝ × 84¾ in. (88 × 217 cm)

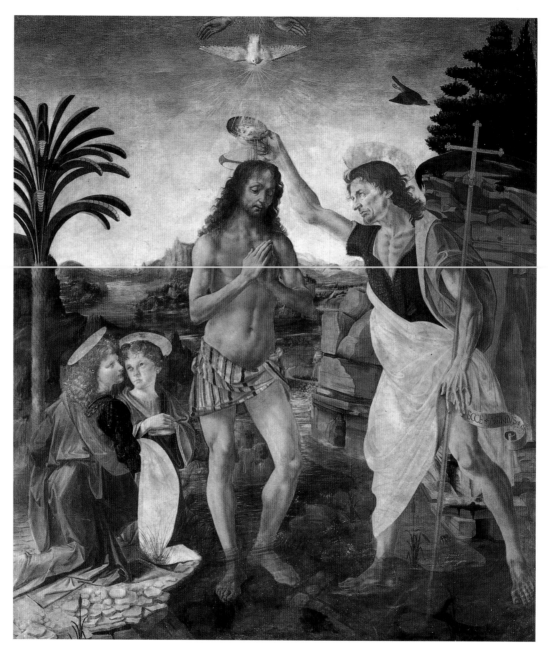

ANDREA VERROCCHIO (1435–1488) and LEONARDO DA VINCI (1452–1519)
The Baptism of Christ, c. 1475
Oil on wood, 70 x 59¼ in. (180 x 152 cm)

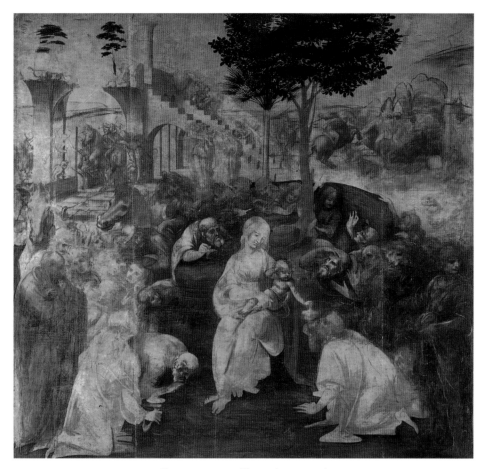

LEONARDO DA VINCI (1452–1519)
The Adoration of the Magi, c. 1481
Tempera and oil on wood, 95 × 96 in. (243 × 246 cm)

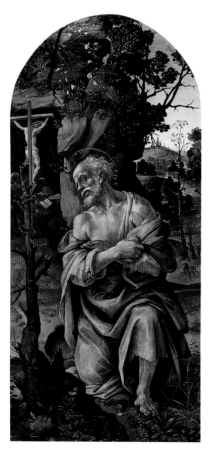

FILIPPINO LIPPI (c. 1457–1504)
Saint Jerome, c. 1485
Oil on wood, 53 × 27¾ in. (136 × 71 cm)

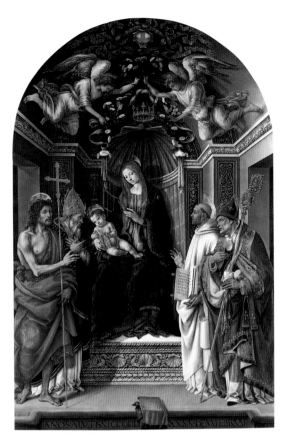

FILIPPINO LIPPI (c. 1457–1504)
Madonna and Child (Madonna of the Otto), 1486
Tempera on wood, 138½ × 99½ in. (355 × 255 cm)

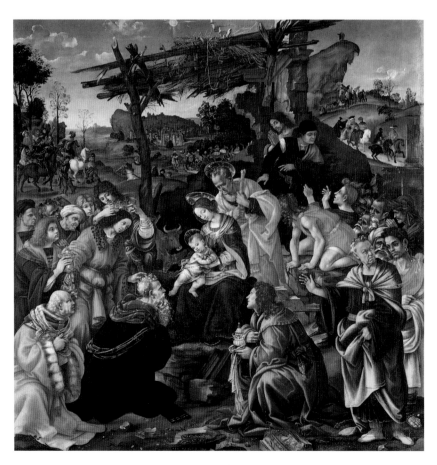

FILIPPINO LIPPI (c. 1457–1504)
The Adoration of the Magi, 1496
Oil on wood, 100 × 95 in. (258 × 243 cm)

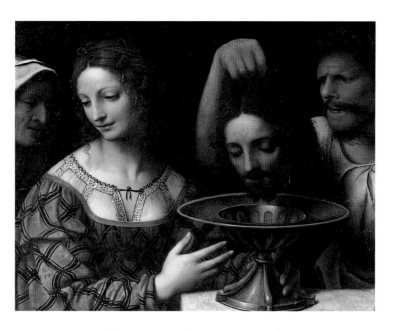

BERNARDINO LUINI (c. 1460–1532)
Executioner with the Head of John the Baptist (Herodias), 1527/31
Tempera on wood, 20 × 22½ in. (51 × 58 cm)

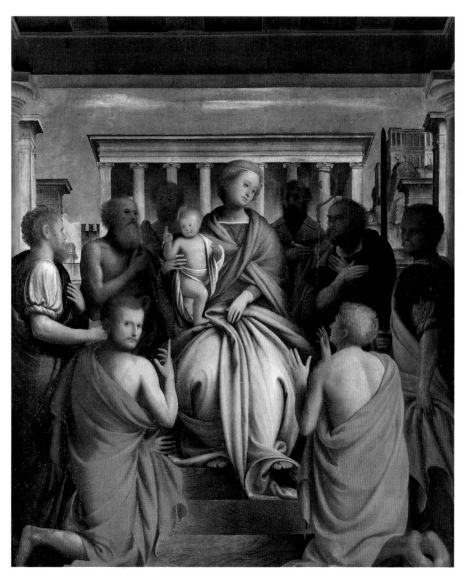

BRAMANTINO (c. 1465–1530)
Madonna and Child with Saints, c. 1520–30
Tempera on wood, 79 × 65 in. (203 × 167 cm)

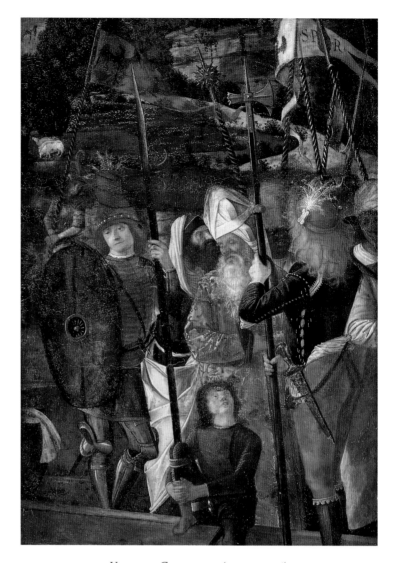

VITTORE CARPACCIO (c. 1450–1526)
Warriors and Old Men, 1493–1500
Oil on wood, 26½ × 16½ in. (68 × 42 cm)

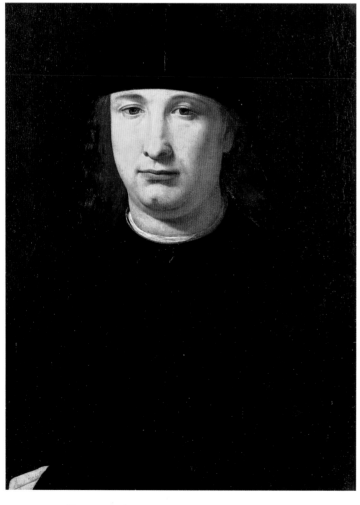

GIOVANNI ANTONIO BOLTRAFFIO (1467–1516)
The Poet Casio, c. 1490–1500
Oil on wood, 20 × 14¼ in. (51.5 × 37 cm)

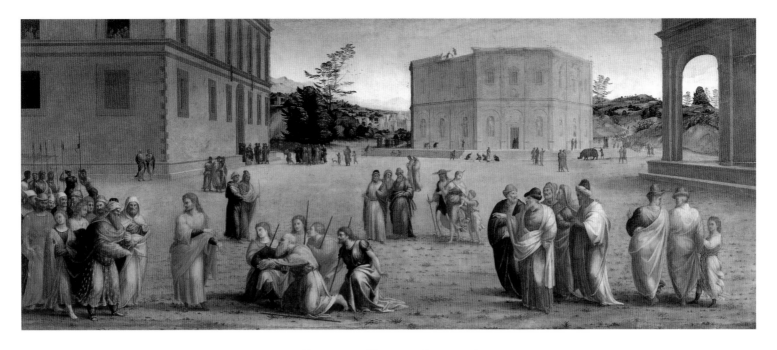

FRANCESCO GRANACCI (1477–1543)
Joseph Presents His Father and Brothers to the Pharaoh, c. 1515
Oil on wood, 37 × 87 in. (95 × 224 cm)

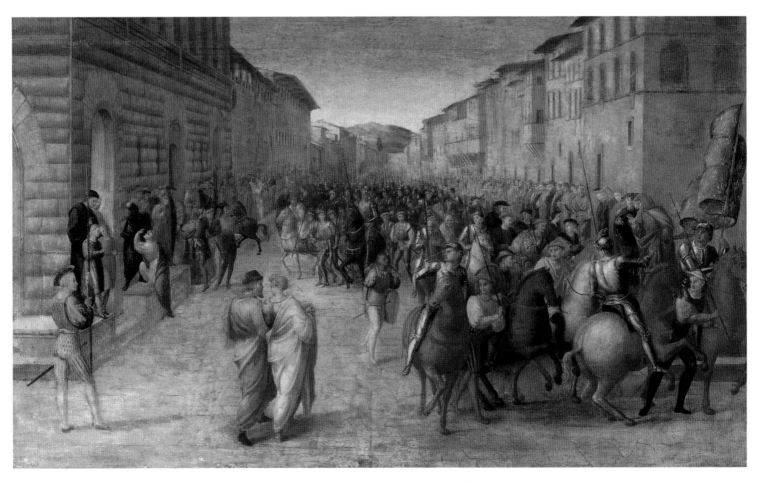

FRANCESCO GRANACCI (1477–1543)
Entry of Charles VIII into Florence, c. 1518
Oil on wood, 30 × 48¼ in. (76 × 122 cm)

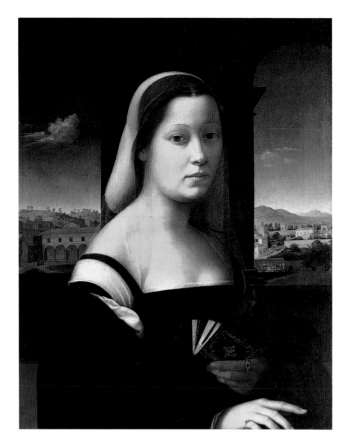

GIULIANO BUGIARDINI (1476–1555)
Portrait of a Woman, 1506–10
Oil on wood, 25⅓ × 18½ in. (65 × 48 cm)

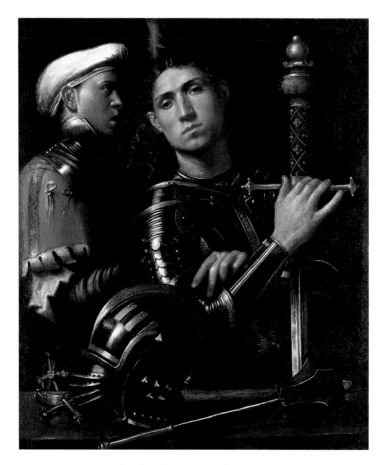

Attributed to GIORGIONE (c. 1477–1510)
Warrior with Shield Bearer, n.d.
Oil on canvas, 35 × 28½ in. (90 × 73 cm)

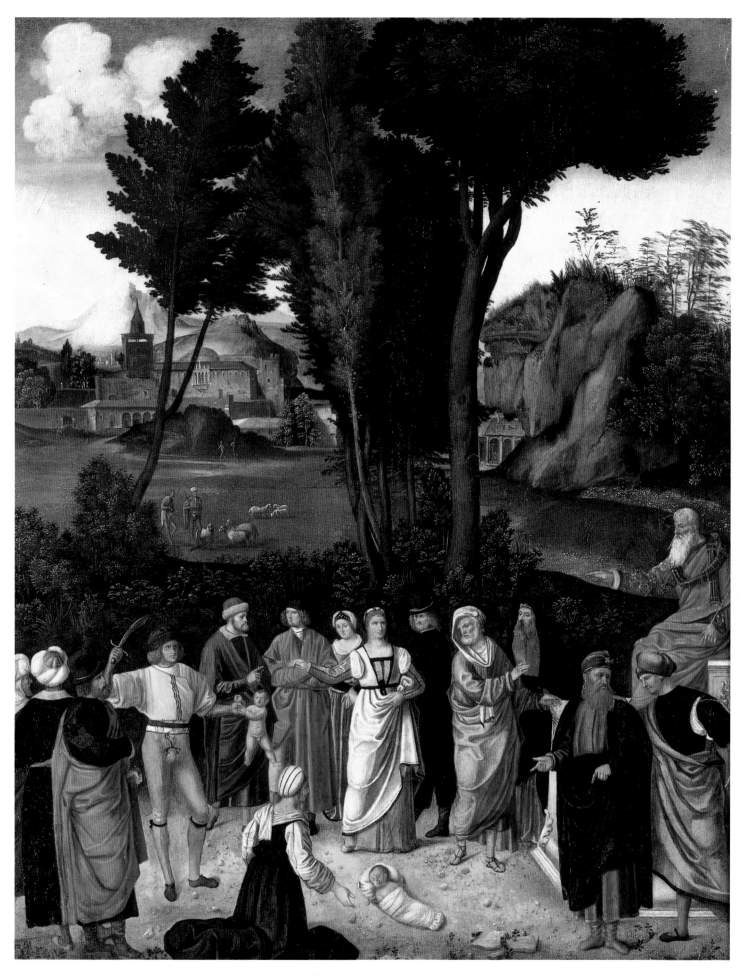

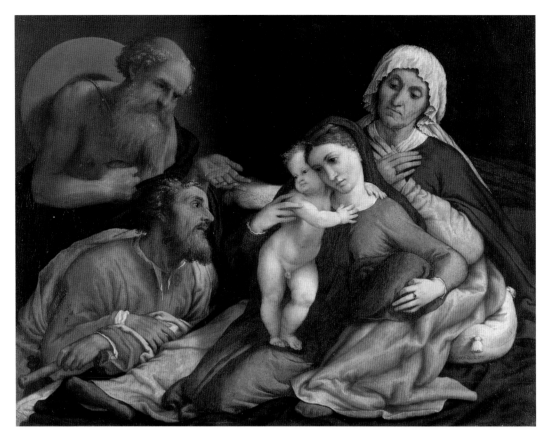

LORENZO LOTTO (c. 1480–1556)
Madonna and Child with Saints, 1534
Oil on canvas, 27 × 34 in. (69 × 87.5 cm)

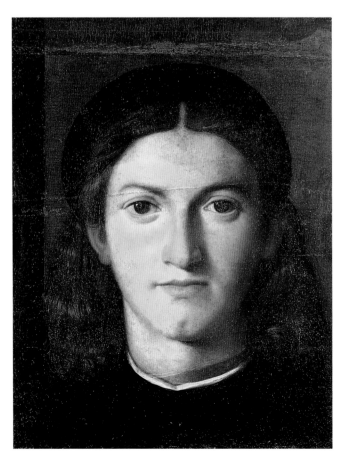

LORENZO LOTTO (c. 1480–1556)
Head of a Young Man, early 1500s
Oil on wood, 11 × 8½ in. (28 × 22 cm)

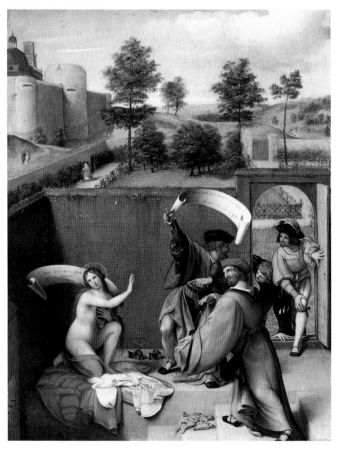

LORENZO LOTTO (c. 1480–1556)
Susanna and the Elders, 1517
Oil on wood, 25¾ × 19½ in. (66 × 50 cm)

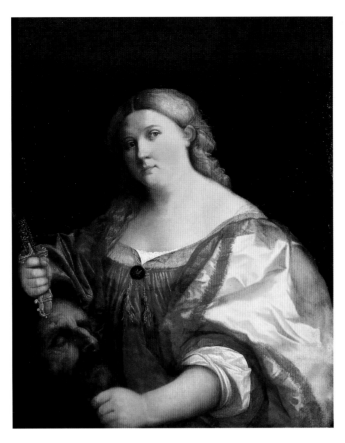

PALMA VECCHIO (c. 1480–1528)
Judith, c. 1525/28
Oil on wood, 35 × 27½ in. (90 × 71 cm)

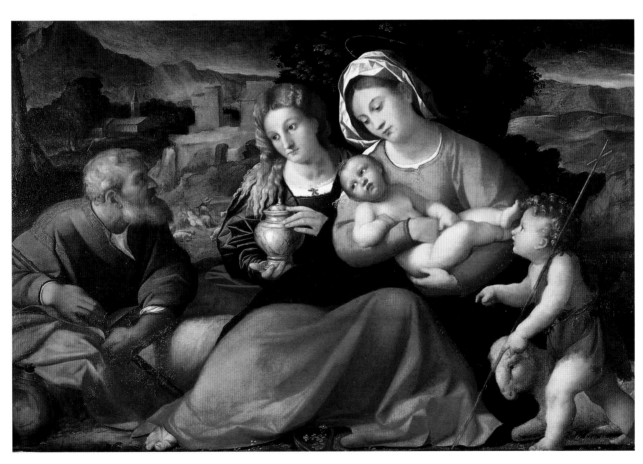

PALMA VECCHIO (c. 1480–1528)
The Holy Family and Saints, early 1550s
Oil on wood, 34 × 45½ in. (87 × 117 cm)

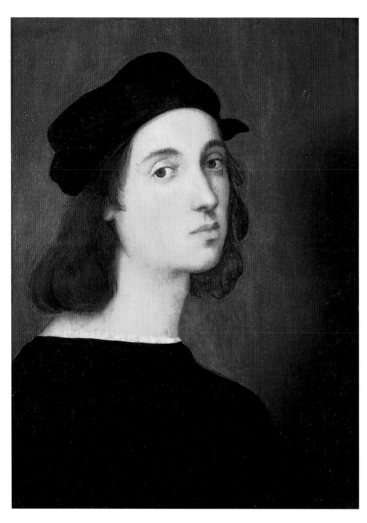

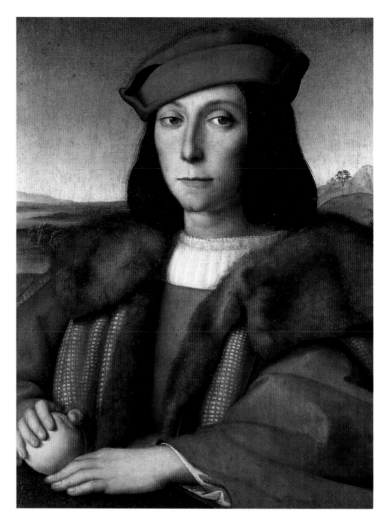

RAPHAEL (1483–1520)
Self-Portrait, c. 1506
Oil on wood, 18½ × 13 in. (47.5 × 33 cm)

RAPHAEL (1483–1520)
*Portrait of an Unknown Man
(Francesco Maria della Rovere?),* 1503/4
Oil on wood, 18¾ × 14 in. (48 × 35.5 cm)

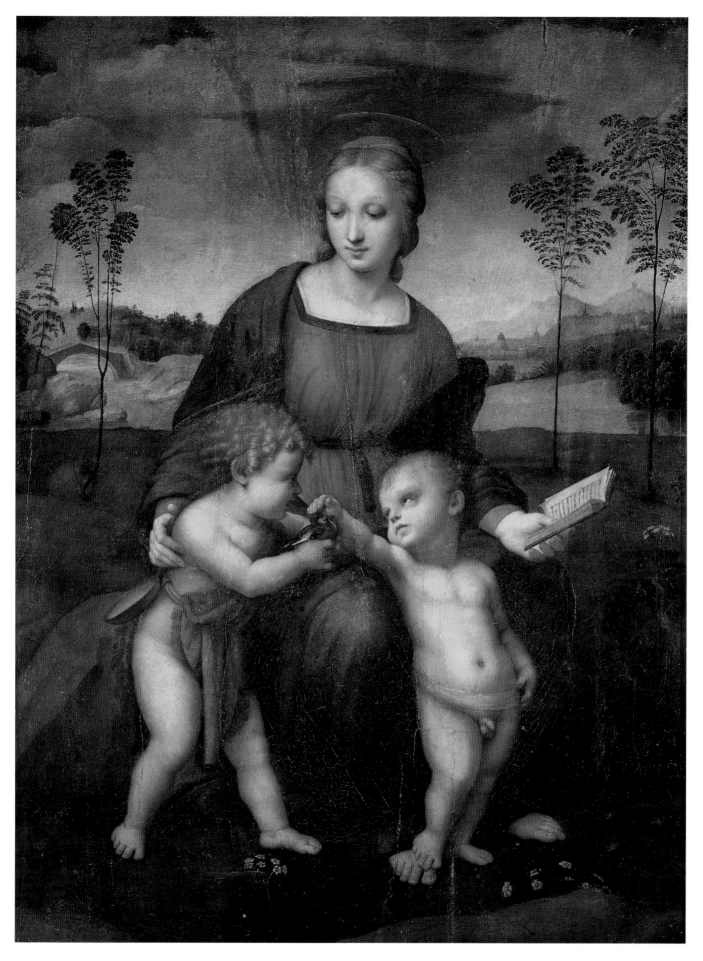

RAPHAEL (1483–1520)
Madonna and Child with Young Saint John
(Madonna del Cardellino), 1505–6
Oil on wood, 41¾ × 30 in. (107 × 77 cm)

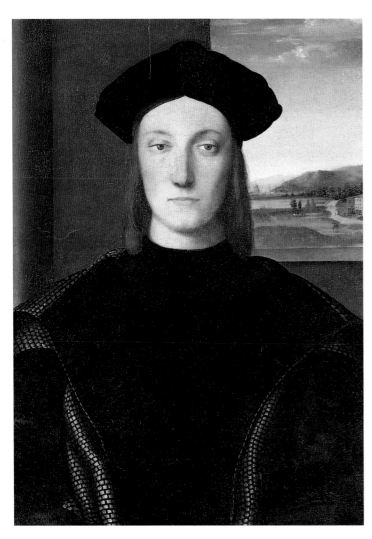

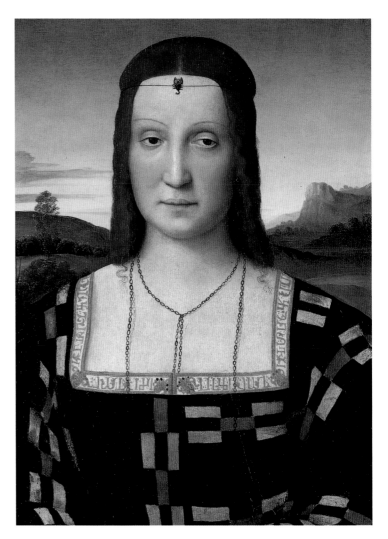

RAPHAEL (1483–1520)
Guidobaldo da Montefeltro, 1506
Oil on wood, 27½ × 19½ in. (70.5 × 49.9 cm)

RAPHAEL (1483–1520)
Elisabetta Gonzaga, 1504–6
Oil on wood, 20½ × 14½ in. (52.5 × 37.3 cm)

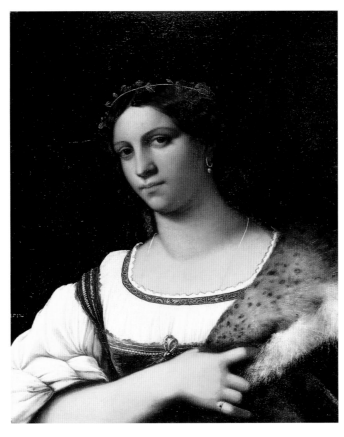

SEBASTIANO DEL PIOMBO (c. 1485–1547)
Portrait of a Woman, 1512
Oil on wood, 26½ × 21½ in. (68 × 55 cm)

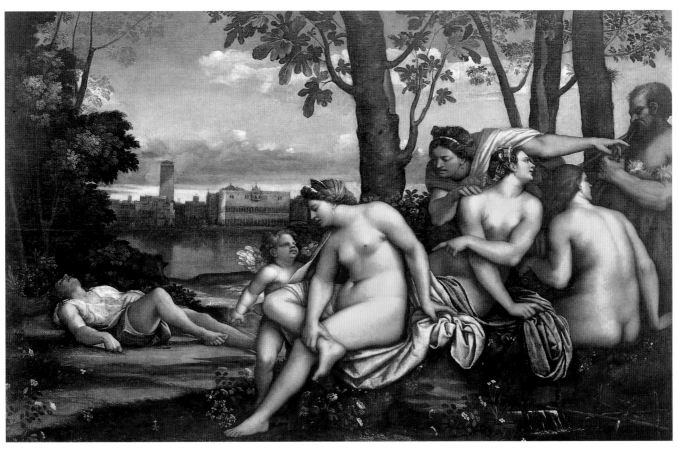

SEBASTIANO DEL PIOMBO (c. 1485–1547)
The Death of Adonis, early 1500s
Oil on canvas, 73½ × 111 in. (189 × 285 cm)

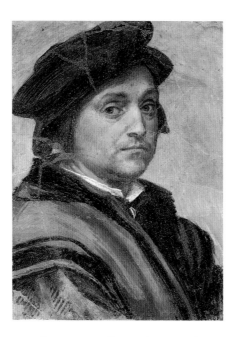

ANDREA DEL SARTO (1486–1531)
Self-Portrait, 1528–30
Fresco on tile, 20 × 14½ in. (51.5 × 37.5 cm)

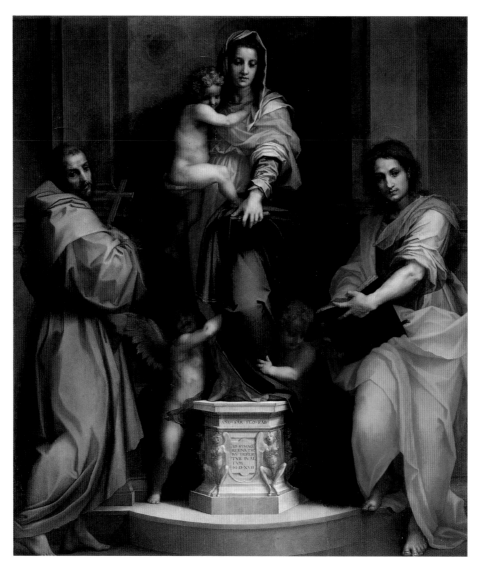

ANDREA DEL SARTO (1486–1531)
Madonna of the Harpies, 1517
Oil on wood, 80¾ × 70 in. (207 × 178 cm)

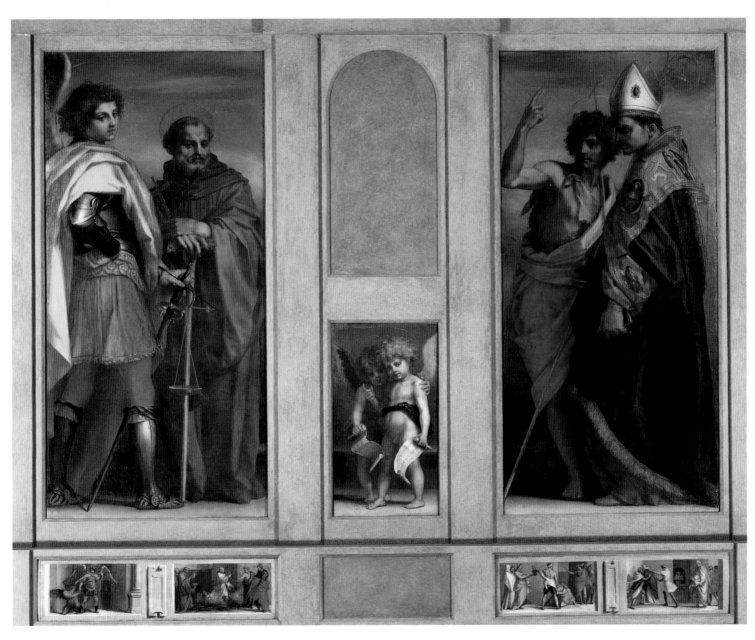

ANDREA DEL SARTO (1486–1531)
Four Saints from an Altarpiece (fragments), 1528
Oil on wood, 71¾ × 67 in. (184 × 172 cm) overall

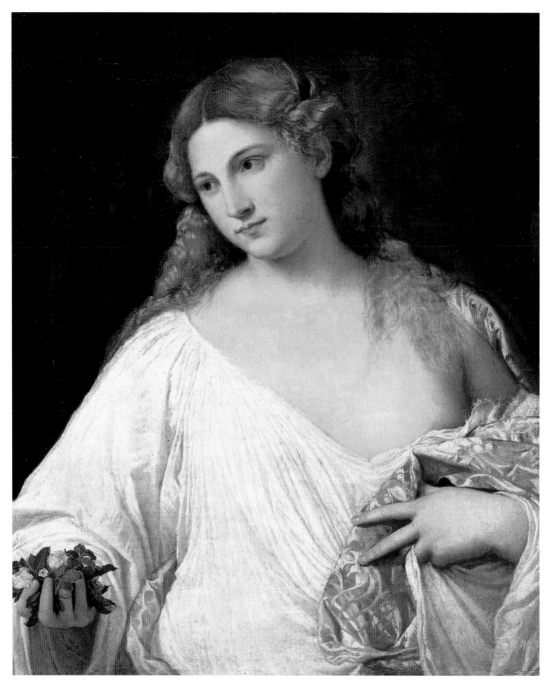

TITIAN (c. 1488–1576)
Flora, c. 1515
Oil on canvas, 31 × 24¾ in. (79.7 × 63.5 cm)

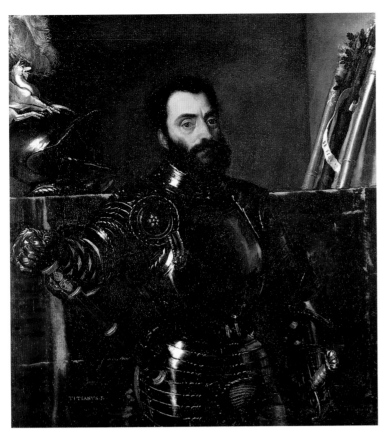

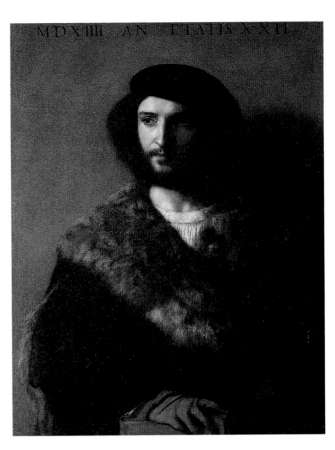

TITIAN (c. 1488–1576)
Francesco Maria della Rovere, 1536–38
Oil on canvas, 44¼ × 40 in. (114 × 103 cm)

TITIAN (c. 1488–1576)
Portrait of the Sick Man, 1514
Oil on canvas, 31½ × 23¼ in. (81 × 60 cm)

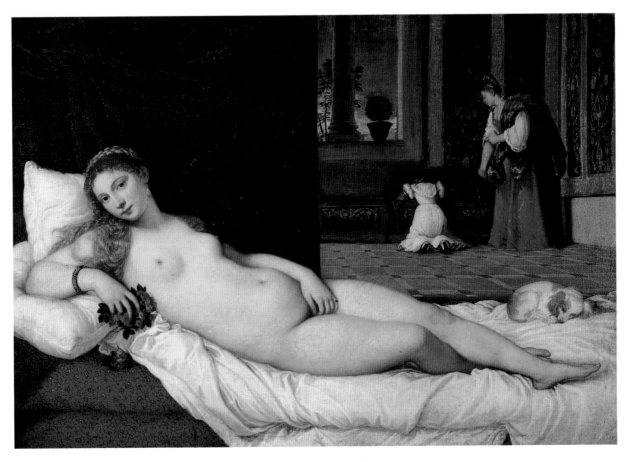

TITIAN (c. 1488–1576)
The Venus of Urbino, c. 1538
Oil on canvas, 46½ × 65 in. (119 × 165 cm)

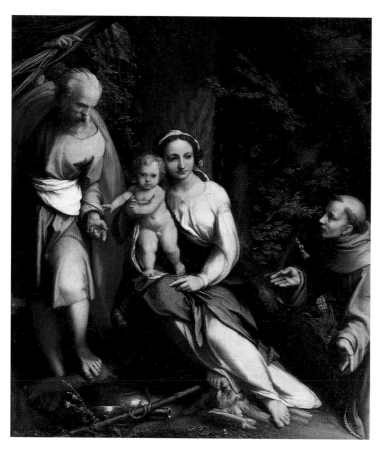

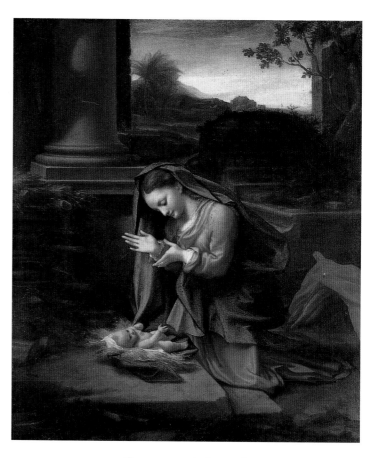

CORREGGIO (1489–1534)
The Rest on the Flight into Egypt, c. 1520
Oil on canvas, 48 × 41½ in. (123.5 × 106.5 cm)

CORREGGIO (1489–1534)
The Adoration of the Child, 1524/26
Oil on canvas, 31½ × 30 in. (81 × 77 cm)

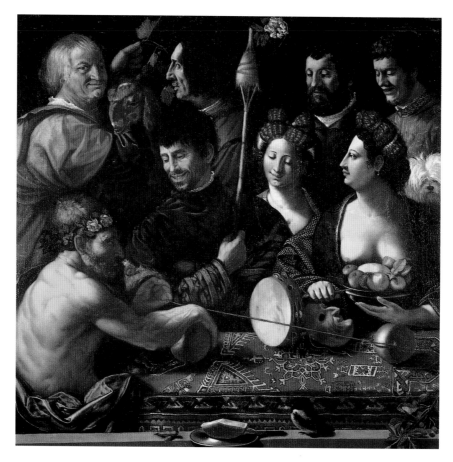

DOSSO DOSSI (1479?–1542)
Witchcraft, 1535–40
Oil on canvas, 56¼ × 56⅝ in. (143 × 144 cm)

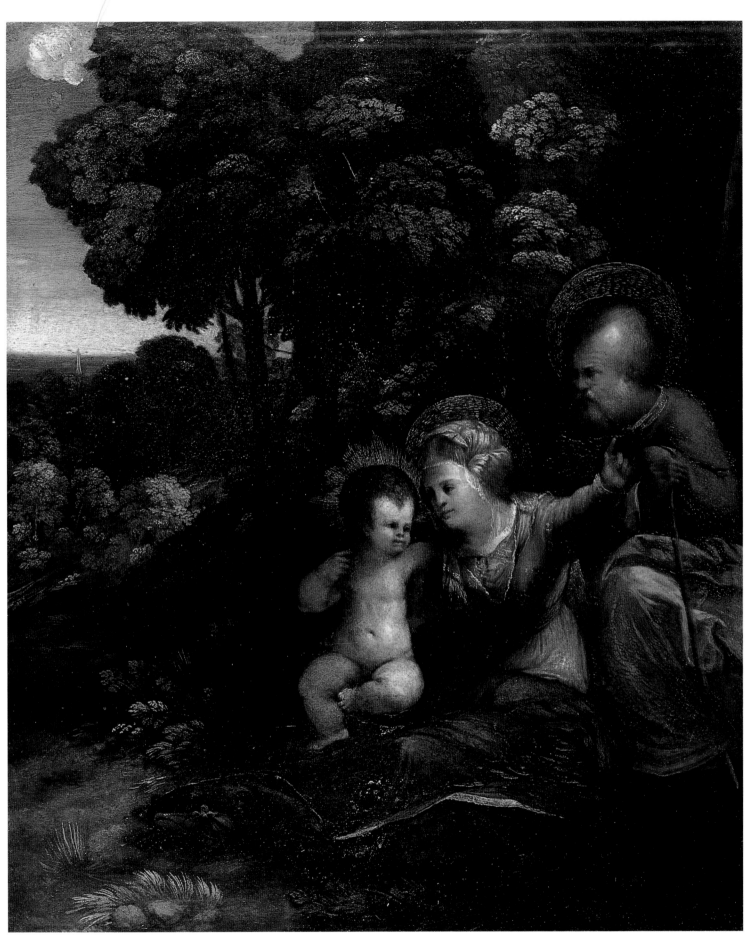

DOSSO DOSSI (1479?–1542)
The Rest on the Flight into Egypt, early 1500s
Tempera on wood, 20¼ × 16½ in. (52 × 42.6 cm)

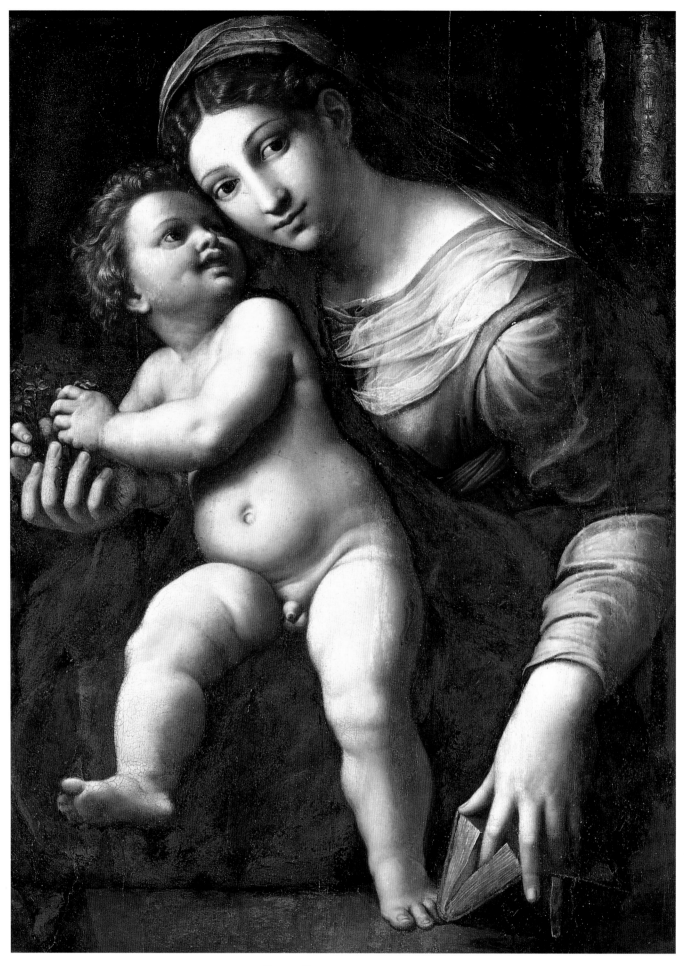

GIULIO ROMANO (c. 1492–1546)
Madonna and Child, 1520/30
Oil on wood, 76 × 30 in. (195 × 77 cm)

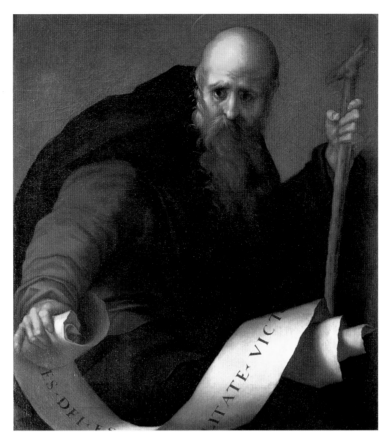

PONTORMO (1494–1556)
Saint Anthony Abbot, c. 1518/19
Oil on wood, 30¾ × 26 in. (78 × 66 cm)

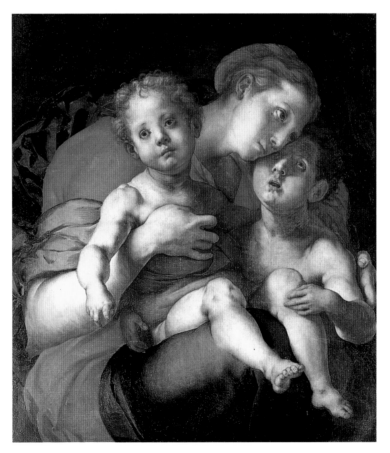

PONTORMO (1494–1556)
Madonna and Child and Young Saint John, 1527/28
Oil on wood, 34½ × 29 in. (89 × 74 cm)

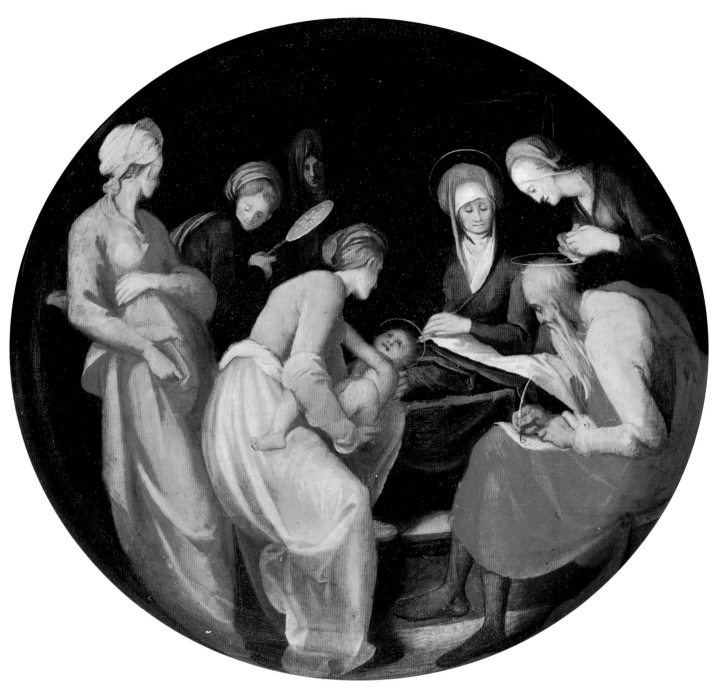

PONTORMO (1494–1556)
The Birth of John the Baptist, 1527
Oil on wood, diameter: 23 in. (59 cm)

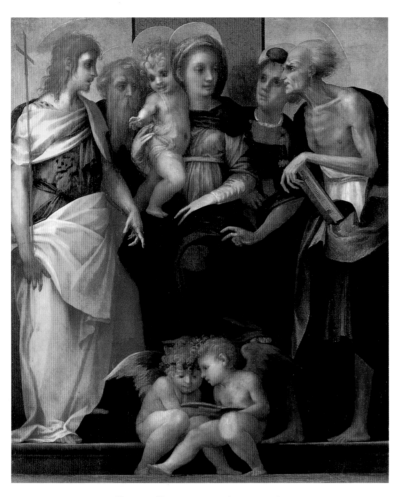

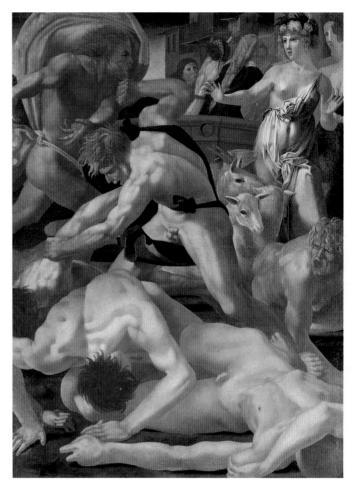

ROSSO FIORENTINO (1495–1540)
Madonna and Child with Saints, 1518
Oil on wood, 55 × 43½ in. (141 × 112 cm)

ROSSO FIORENTINO (1495–1540)
Moses Defending the Daughters of Jethro, c. 1523
Oil on canvas, 62¼ × 46 in. (160 × 117 cm)

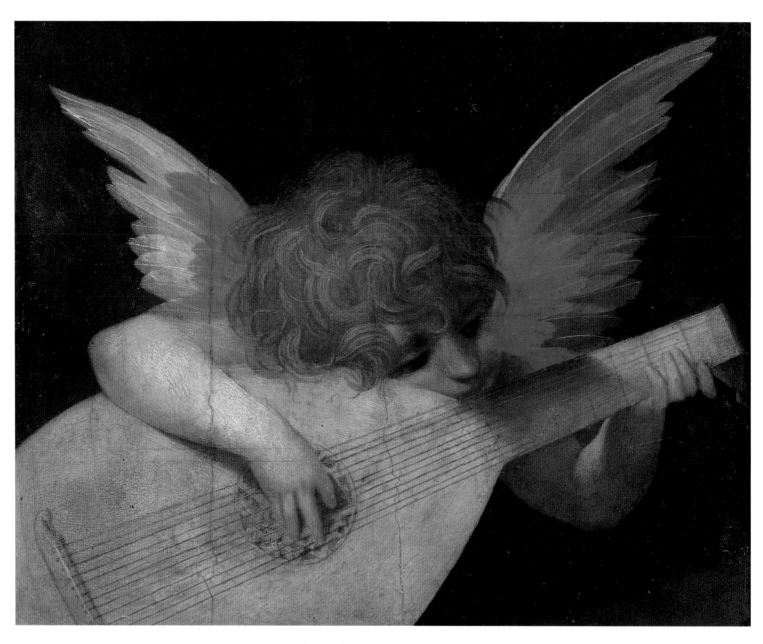

ROSSO FIORENTINO (1495–1540)
Musical Angel, c. 1522
Oil on wood, 15¼ × 18⅓ in. (39 × 47 cm)

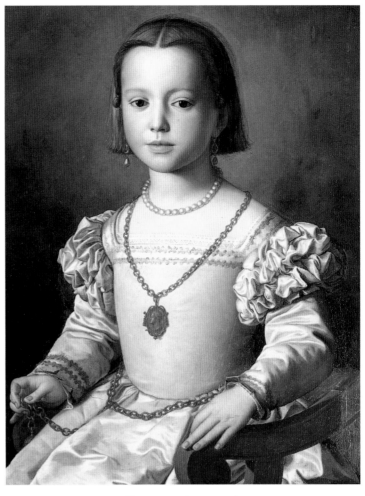

BRONZINO (1503–1572)
Bia, Illegitimate Daughter of Cosimo I de' Medici, before 1542
Oil on wood, 24½ × 19 in. (63 × 48 cm)

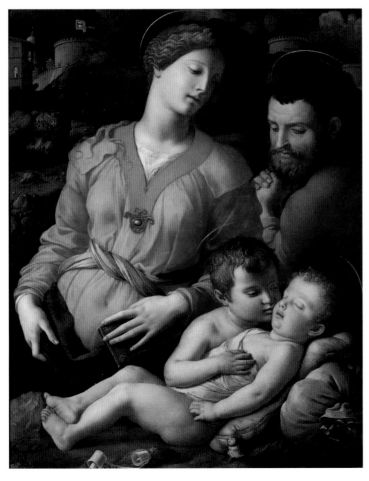

BRONZINO (1503–1572)
The Panciatichi Holy Family, c. 1540
Oil on wood, 45½ × 34 in. (117 × 89 cm)

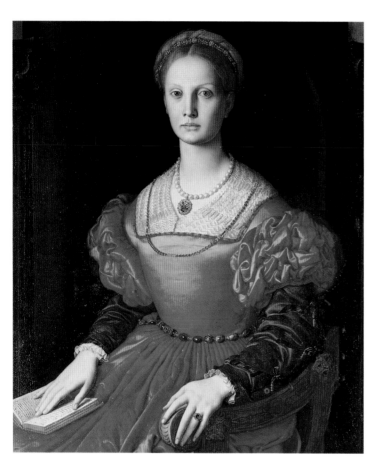

BRONZINO (1503–1572)
Lucrezia Panciatichi, c. 1540
Oil on wood, 39¾ × 33 in. (102 × 85 cm)

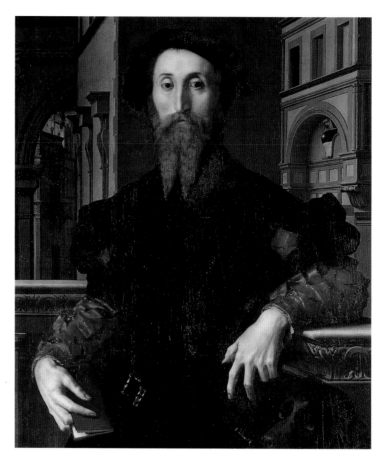

BRONZINO (1503–1572)
Bartolomeo Panciatichi, n.d.
Oil on wood, 40½ × 32¾ in. (104 × 84 cm)

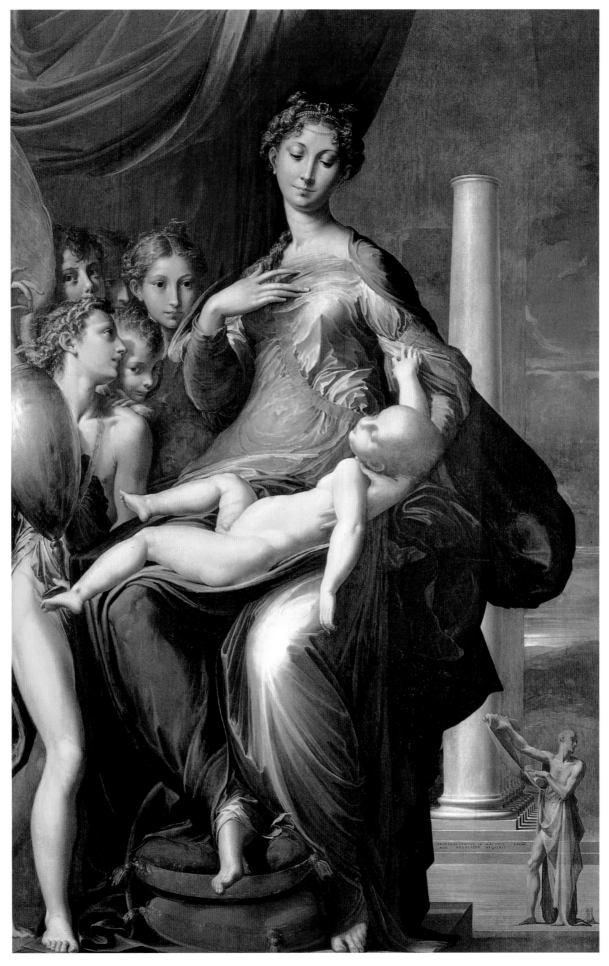

PARMIGIANINO (1503–1540)
Madonna with the Long Neck, 1534–40
Oil on wood, 85¼ × 52½ in. (219 × 135 cm)

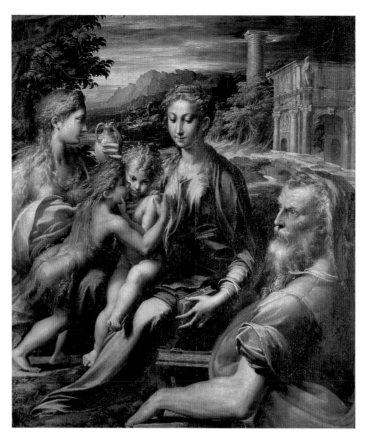

PARMIGIANINO (1503–1540)
Madonna of Saint Zachariah, c. 1527–30
Oil on wood, 28½ × 23½ in. (73 × 60 cm)

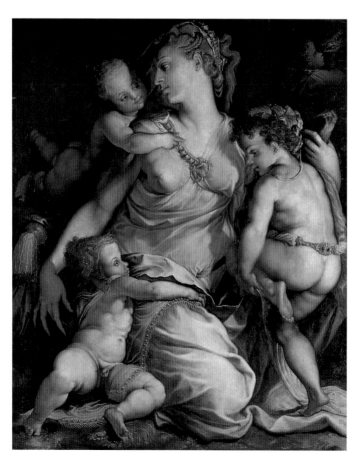

FRANCESCO DE ROSSI SALVIATI (1510–1563)
Charity, 1544–48
Oil on wood, 61 × 47½ in. (156 × 122 cm)

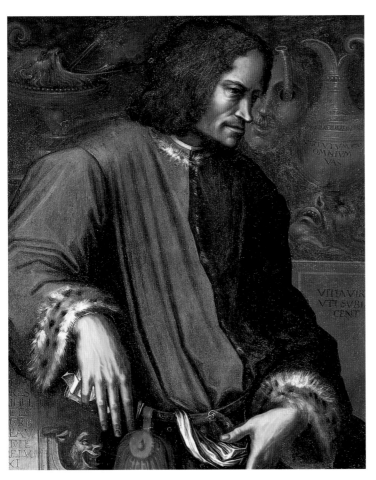

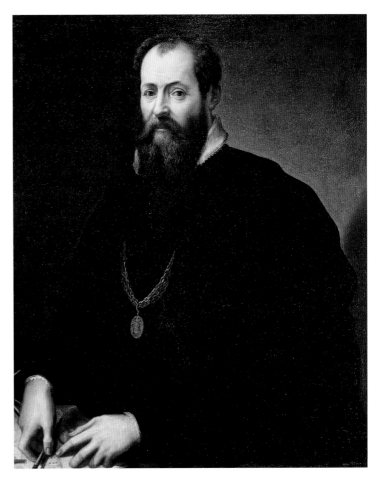

GIORGIO VASARI (1511–1574)
Lorenzo the Magnificent, 1534
Oil on wood, 35 × 28 in. (90 × 72 cm)

GIORGIO VASARI (1511–1574)
Self-Portrait, n.d.
Oil on wood, 39 × 31 in. (100.5 × 80 cm)

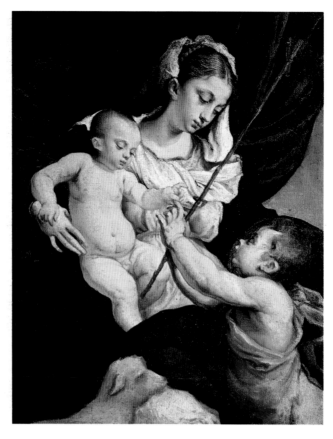

JACOPO BASSANO (c. 1517–1592)
Madonna and Child with Saint John the Baptist, c. 1570
Oil on canvas, 31 × 23¼ in. (79 × 60 cm)

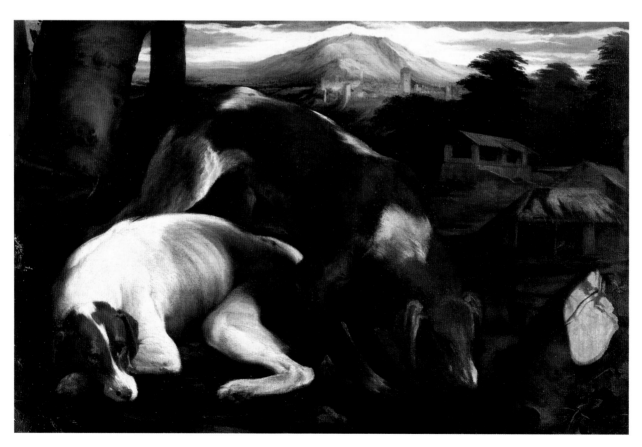

JACOPO BASSANO (c. 1517–1592)
Hunting Dogs, c. 1560
Oil on canvas, 33 × 49 in. (85 × 126 cm)

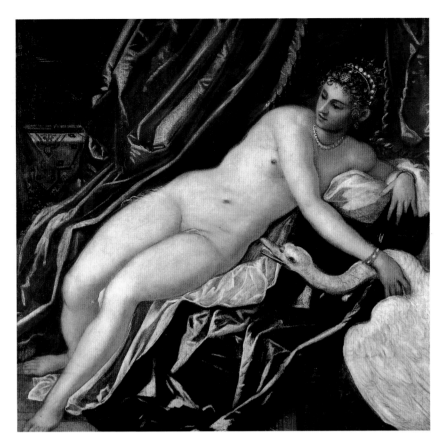

TINTORETTO (1518–1594)
Leda and the Swan, c. 1550–60
Oil on canvas, 63 × 85 in. (162 × 218 cm)

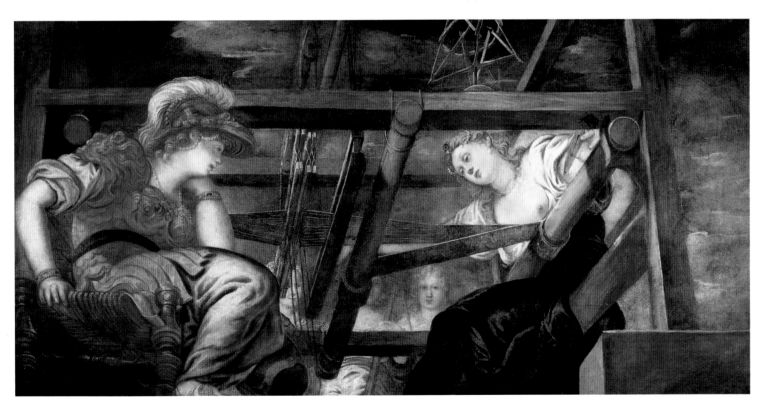

TINTORETTO (1518–1594)
Minerva and Arachne, c. 1570–80
Oil on canvas, 56½ × 106 in. (145 × 272 cm)

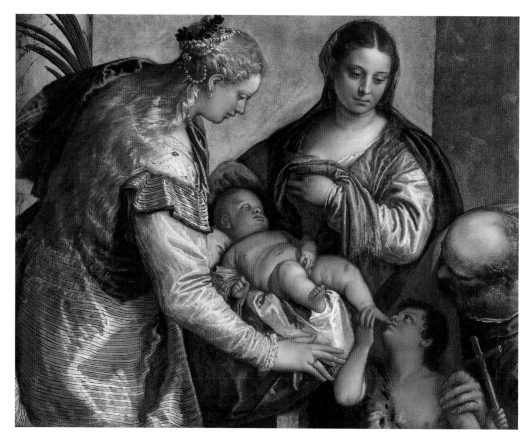

PAOLO VERONESE (1528–1588)
The Holy Family with Saint Barbara and Young Saint John, 1550/65
Oil on canvas, 33½ × 47½ in. (86 × 122 cm)

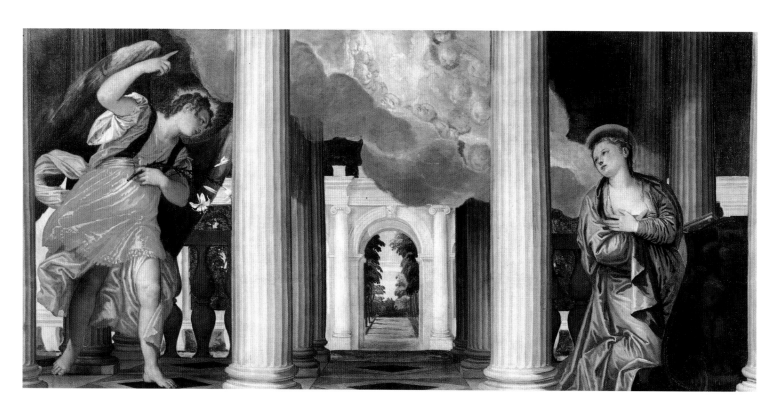

PAOLO VERONESE (1528–1588)
The Annunciation, 1550–60
Oil on canvas, 55¾ × 111½ in. (143 × 291 cm)

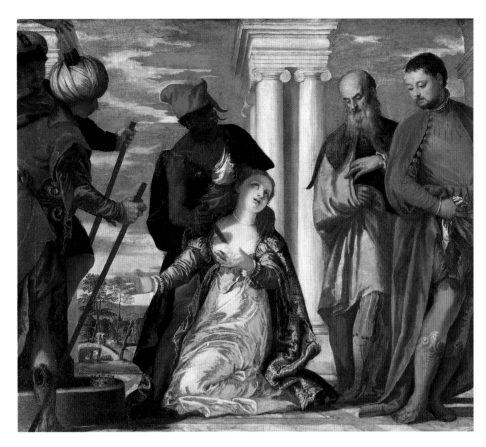

PAOLO VERONESE (1528–1588)
The Martyrdom of Saint Justina, 1570–80
Oil on canvas, 40 × 44 in. (103 × 113 cm)

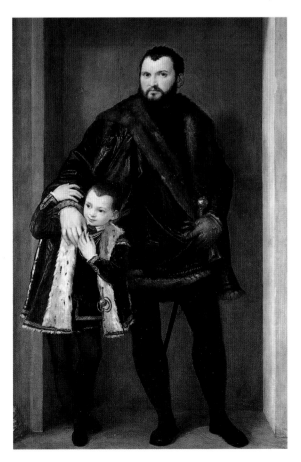

PAOLO VERONESE (1528–1588)
The Count da Porto with His Son, 1550–60
Oil on canvas, 96⅓ × 52 in. (247 × 133 cm)

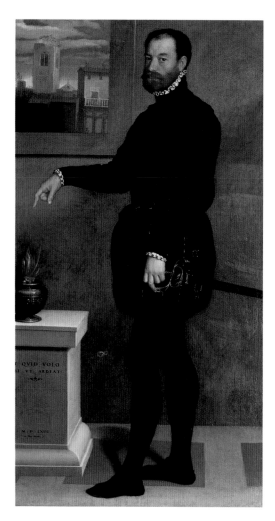

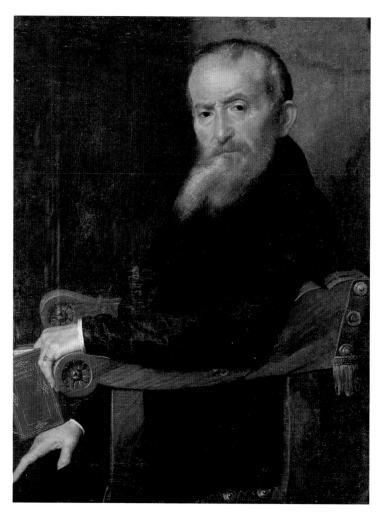

GIOVANNI BATTISTA MORONI (c. 1525–1578)
The Count Pietro Secco-Suardo, 1563
Oil on canvas, 72 × 40½ in. (183 × 104 cm)

GIOVANNI BATTISTA MORONI (c. 1525–1578)
Giovanni Antonio Pantera, n.d.
Oil on canvas, 31½ × 24½ in. (81 × 63 cm)

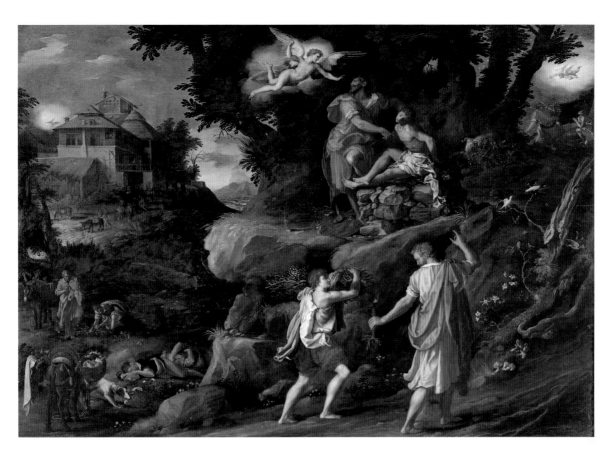

ALESSANDRO ALLORI (1535–1607)
The Sacrifice of Isaac, 1601
Oil on wood, 36½ × 51 in. (94 × 131 cm)

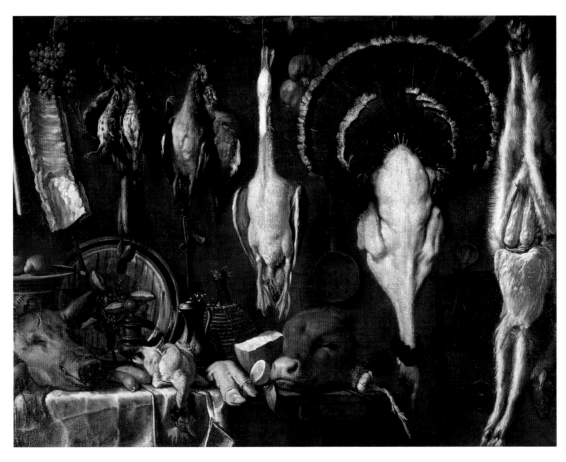

EMPOLI (JACOPO CHIMENTI) (1551–1646)
Still Life, 1624
Oil on canvas, 46½ × 59¼ in. (119 × 152 cm)

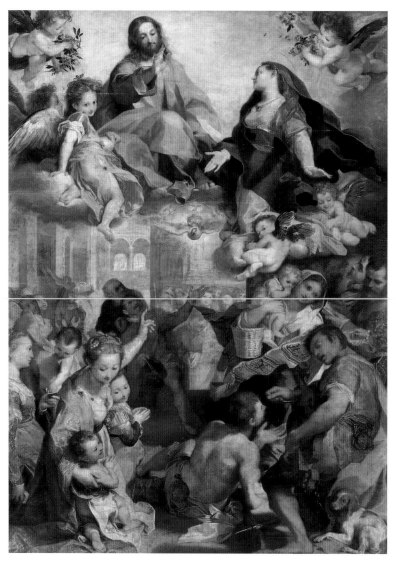

FEDERICO BAROCCI (1535–1612)
Madonna of the People, 1575–79
Oil on wood, 140 × 99 in. (359 × 252 cm)

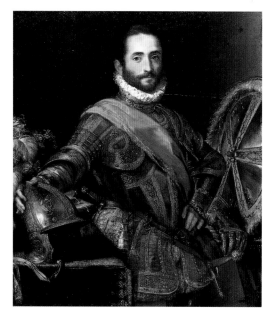

FEDERICO BAROCCI (1535–1612)
Francesco II della Rovere, 1572
Oil on canvas, 44 × 36¼ in. (113 × 93 cm)

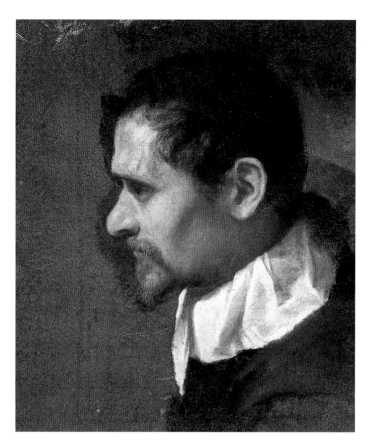

ANNIBALE CARRACCI (1560–1609)
Self-Portrait in Profile, 1590–1600
Oil on canvas, 17 ¾ × 14 ¾ in. (45.5 × 37.9 cm)

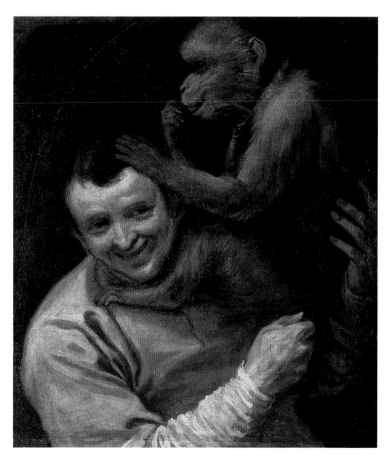

ANNIBALE CARRACCI (1560–1609)
Man with a Monkey, 1590–91
Oil on canvas, 26 ½ × 22 ¾ in. (68 × 58.3 cm)

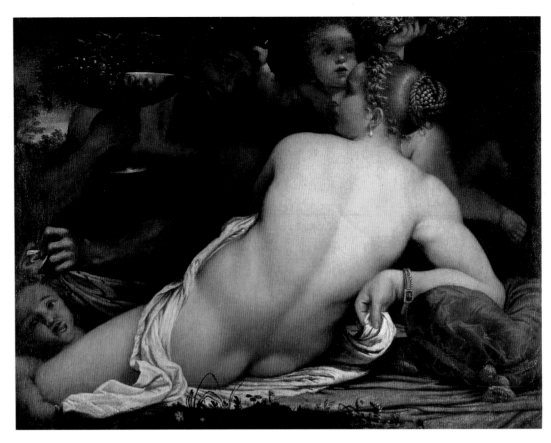

ANNIBALE CARRACCI (1560–1609)
Venus with Satyr and Cupids, 1588
Oil on paper, 43½ × 55⅞ in. (112 × 142 cm)

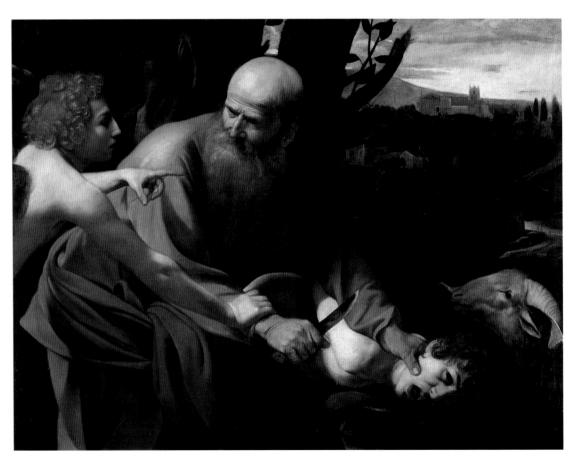

MICHELANGELO MERISI DA CARAVAGGIO (1573–1610)
The Sacrifice of Isaac, 1590/1610
Oil on canvas, 40½ × 52½ in. (104 × 135 cm)

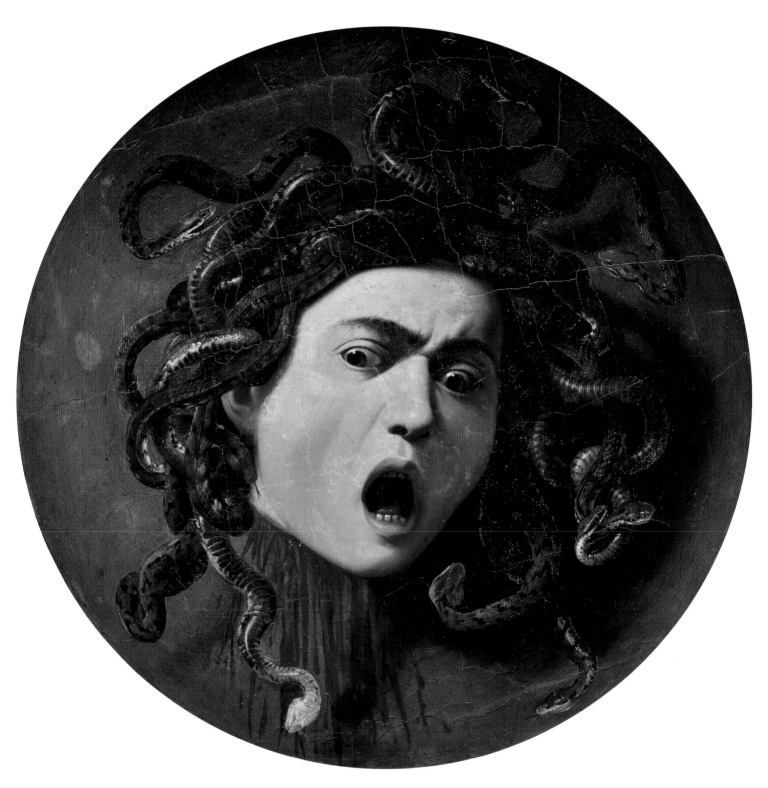

MICHELANGELO MERISI DA CARAVAGGIO (1573–1610)
Medusa, after 1590
Oil on canvas mounted on wood, diameter: 21½ in. (55 cm)

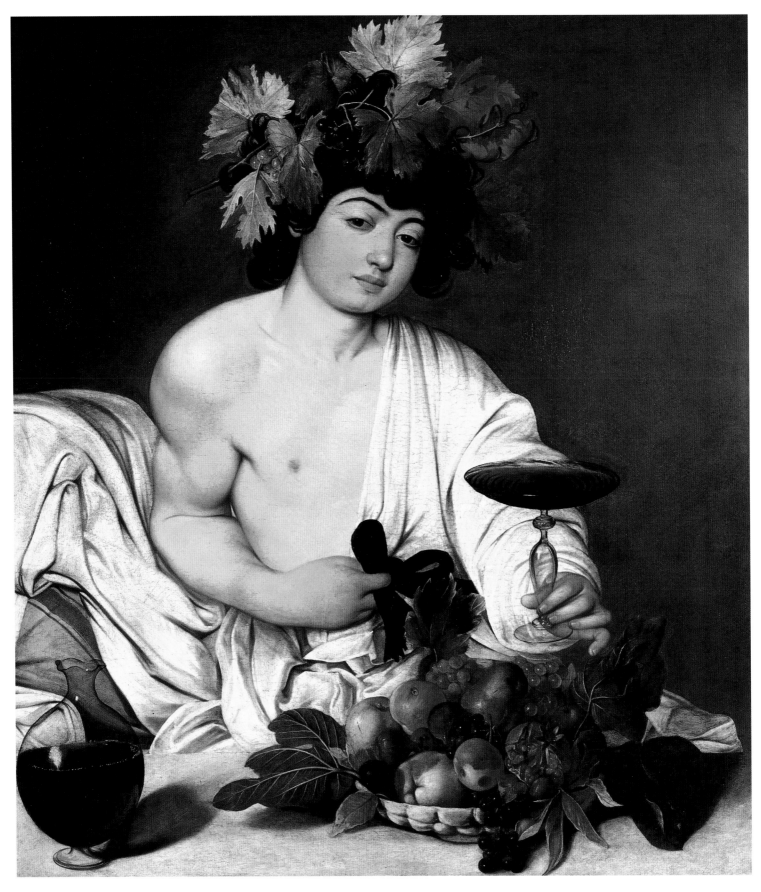

MICHELANGELO MERISI DA CARAVAGGIO (1573–1610)
Young Bacchus, 1588–89
Oil on canvas, 37 × 33 in. (95 × 85 cm)

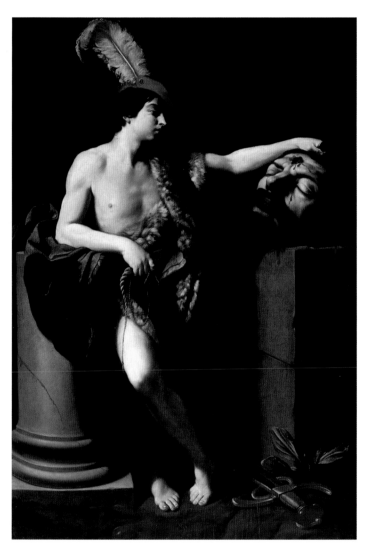

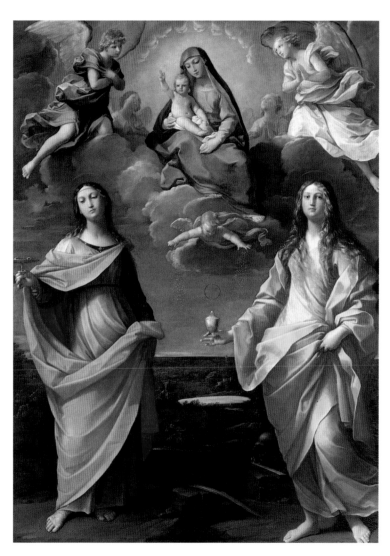

GUIDO RENI (1575–1642)
David with the Head of Goliath, 1605
Oil on canvas, 86½ × 57⅓ in. (222 × 147 cm)

GUIDO RENI (1575–1642)
Madonna of the Snow, c. 1625
Oil on canvas, 109 × 68½ in. (280 × 176 cm)

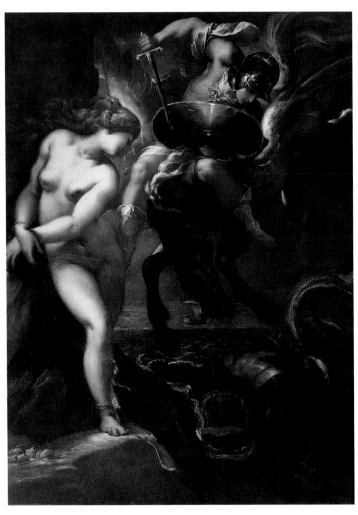

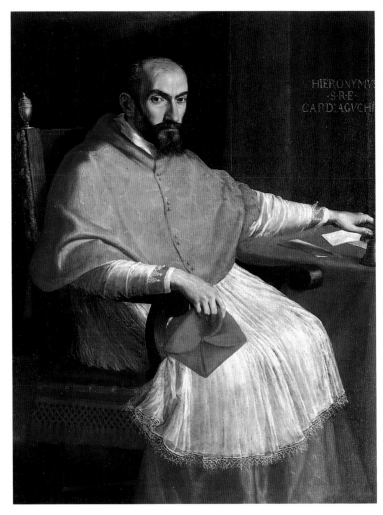

MORAZZONE (PIER FRANCESCO MAZZUCCHELLI) (1573–1626)
Perseus and Andromeda, c. 1610
Oil on canvas, 46¼ × 36 in. (119 × 92.5 cm)

DOMENICHINO (1581–1641)
Cardinal Agucchi, 1605
Oil on canvas, 55⅞ × 44⅛ in. (142 × 112 cm)

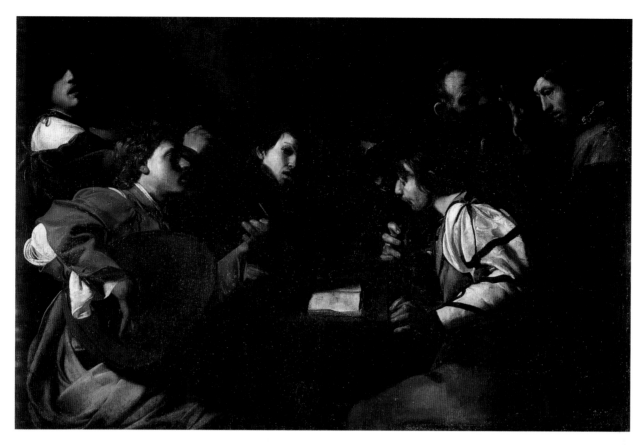

BARTOLOMEO MANFREDI (c. 1587–1620/21)
Concert, 1610–20
Oil on canvas, 50 × 74 in. (130 × 189.5 cm)

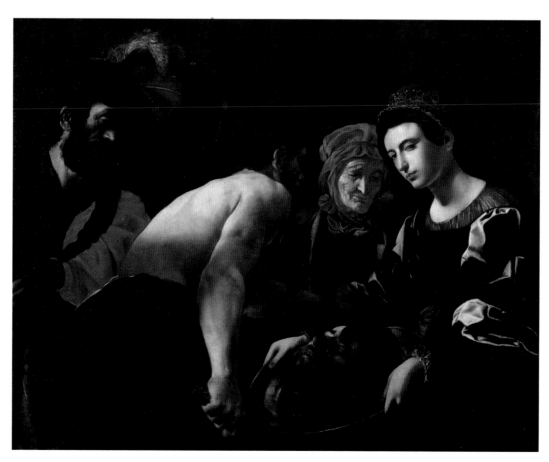

BATTISTELLO CARACCIOLO (d. 1637)
Salome, c. 1615–20
Oil on canvas, 51½ × 61 in. (132 × 156 cm)

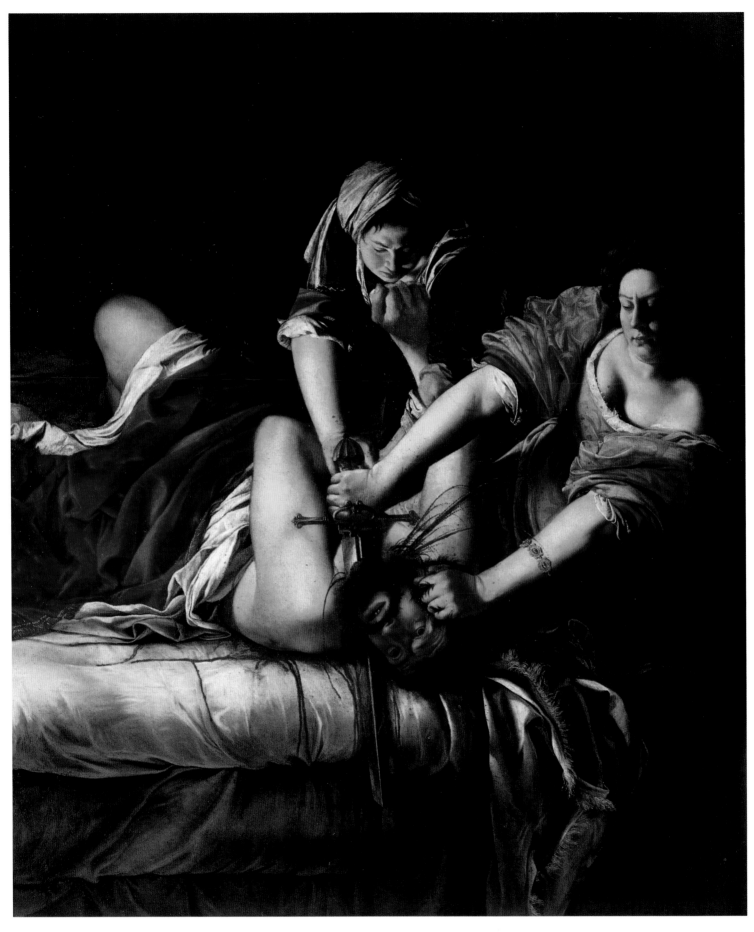

ARTEMISIA GENTILESCHI (1593–1652)
Judith and Holofernes, c. 1620
Oil on canvas, 77½ × 63 in. (199 × 162.5 cm)

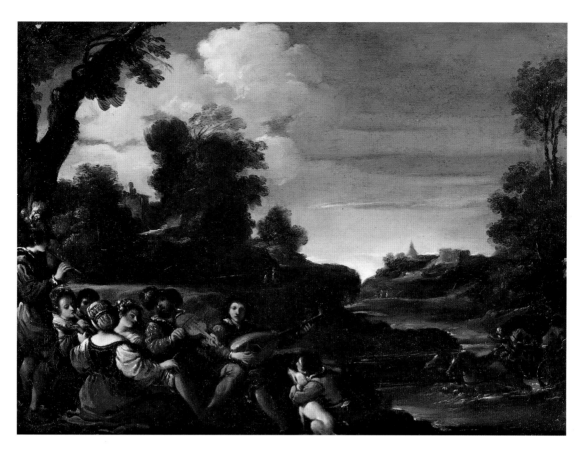

GUERCINO (1591–1666)
Summer Diversions, c. 1617
Oil on copper, 13¼ × 18 in. (34 × 46 cm)

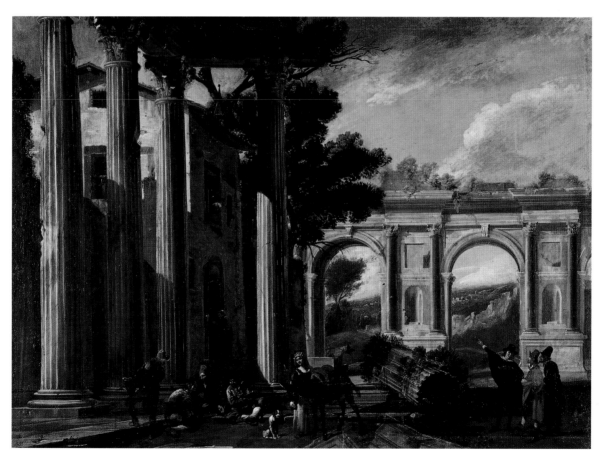

VIVIANO CODAZZI (1604–1670)
Architectural View, c. 1627
Oil on canvas, 28½ × 38¼ in. (73 × 98 cm)

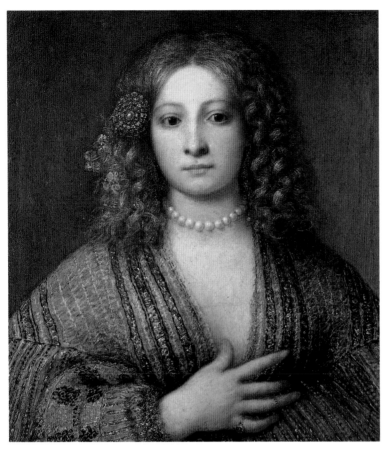

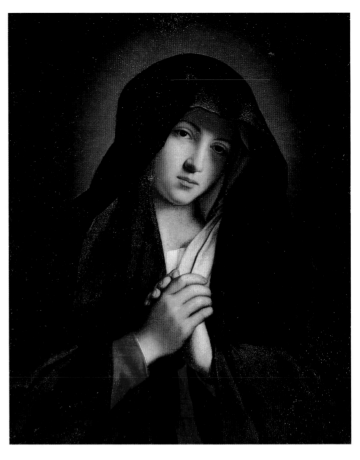

GIROLAMO FORABOSCO (1604–1679)
Portrait of a Courtesan, c. 1665
Oil on canvas, 26⅛ × 20⅞ in. (66.5 × 53 cm)

SASSOFERRATO (GIOVANNI BATTISTA SALVI) (1609–1685)
Our Lady of Sorrows, 1680–85
Oil on canvas, 24 × 22½ in. (62 × 58 cm)

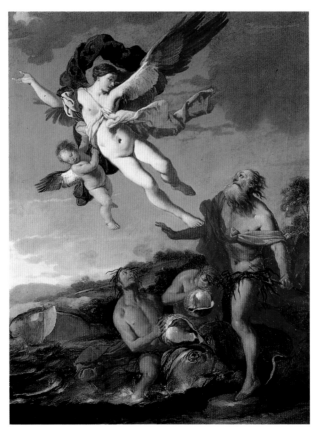

GIULIO CARPIONI (1613–1679)
Neptune Chasing Coronis, 1665/70
Oil on canvas, 26 × 19½ in. (67 × 50 cm)

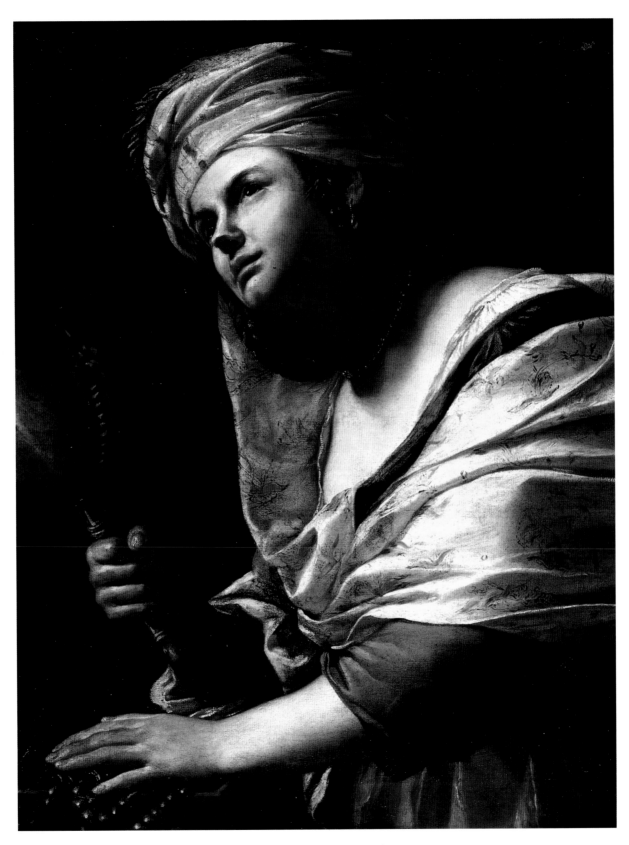

MATTIA PRETI (1613–1699)
Vanity, c. 1650–70
Oil on canvas, 36½ × 25⅝ in. (93.5 × 65 cm)

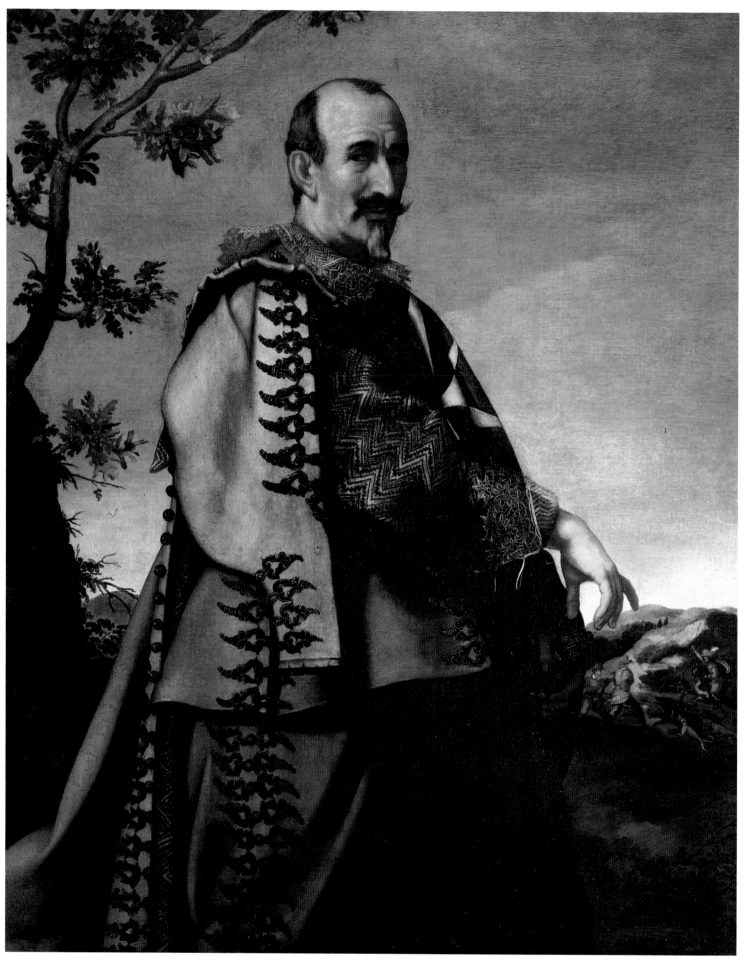

CARLO DOLCI (1616–1686)
Ainolfo de' Bardi, 1632
Oil on canvas, 58⅞ × 46½ in. (149.5 × 119 cm)

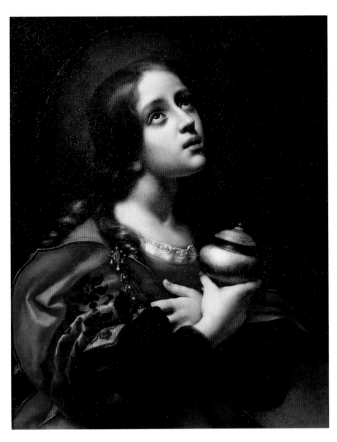

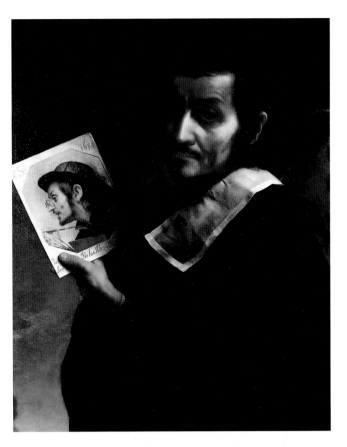

CARLO DOLCI (1616–1686)
Magdalene, 1660/70
Oil on canvas, 28½ × 22 in. (73.5 × 56.5 cm)

CARLO DOLCI (1616–1686)
Self-Portrait, 1674
Oil on canvas, 29 × 23½ in. (74.5 × 60.5 cm)

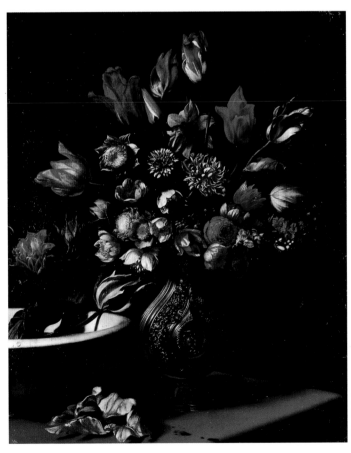

CARLO DOLCI (1616–1686)
Flowers, 1665/75
Oil on canvas, 27 × 21½ in. (70 × 55 cm)

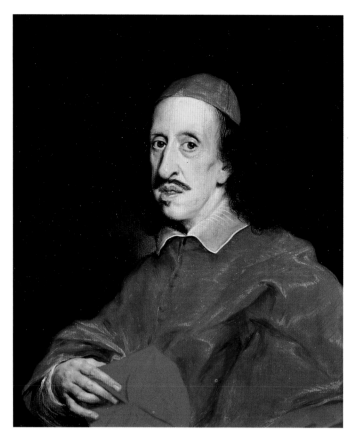

BACICCIO (GIOVANNI BATTISTA GAULLI) (1639–1709)
Cardinal Leopoldo de' Medici, c. 1667
Oil on canvas, 28½ × 23 in. (73 × 60 cm)

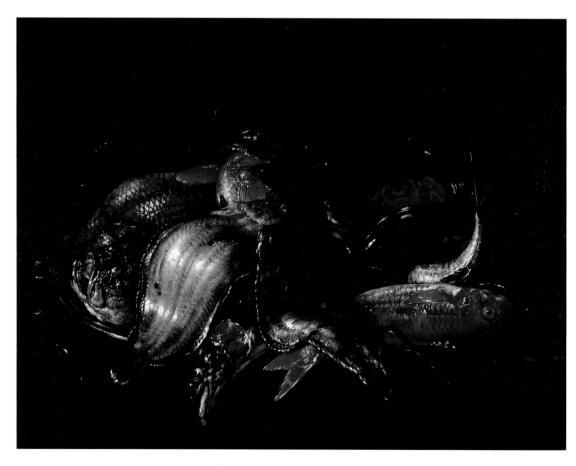

GIUSEPPE RECCO (1634–1695)
Still Life with Fish, 1691
Oil on canvas, 49½ × 59½ in. (127 × 153 cm)

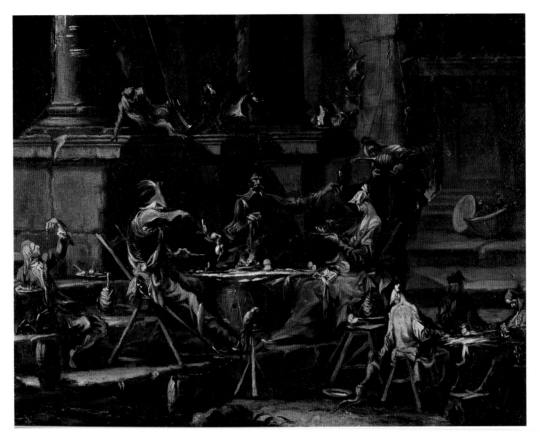

ALESSANDRO MAGNASCO (c. 1667–1747)
The Gypsies' Meal, c. 1710
Oil on canvas, 22 × 28 in. (56 × 71 cm)

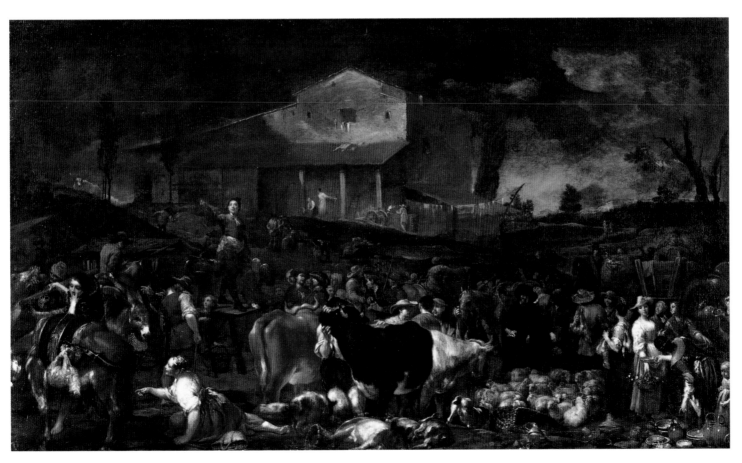

GIUSEPPE MARIA CRESPI (1665–1747)
The Fair at Poggio a Caiano, 1709
Oil on canvas, 45½ × 76½ in. (116.7 × 196.3 cm)

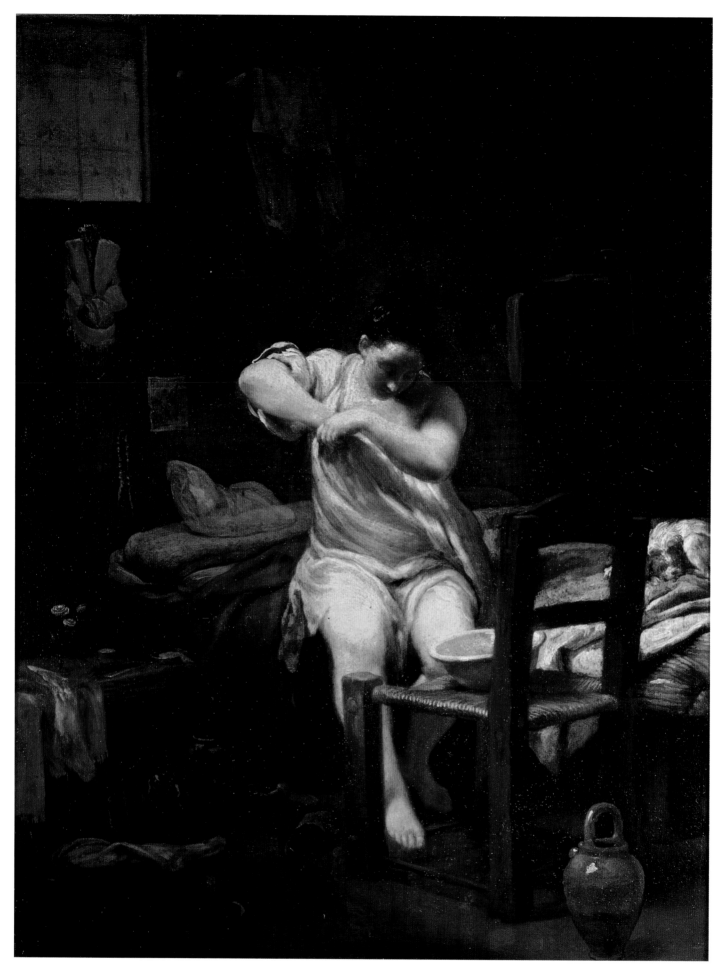

GIUSEPPE MARIA CRESPI (1665–1747)
The Flea, 1710–30
Oil on copper, 18 × 13¼ in. (46.3 × 34 cm)

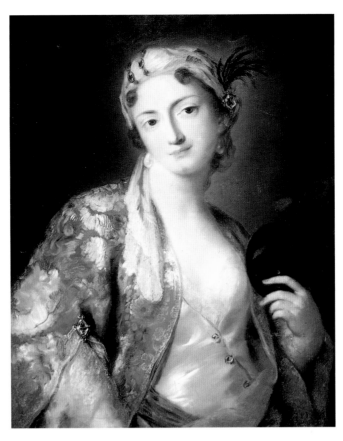

ROSALBA CARRIERA (1675–1757)
Felicità Sartori(?), 1730–40
Pastel on canvas, 27 × 21½ in. (70 × 55 cm)

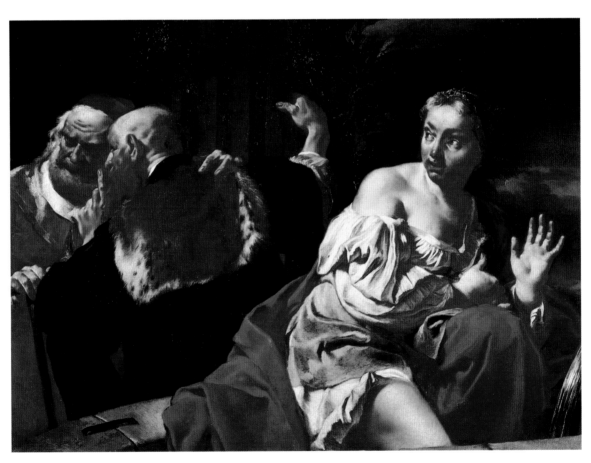

GIOVANNI BATTISTA PIAZZETTA (1682–1754)
Susanna and the Elders, before 1720
Oil on canvas, 39 × 52½ in. (100 × 135 cm)

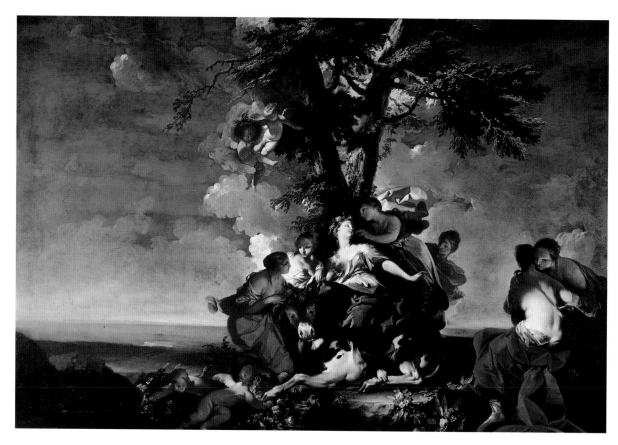

GIOVANNI DOMENICO FERRETTI (1692–1747)
The Rape of Europa, 1720–40
Oil on canvas, 57⅞ × 80 in. (147 × 205 cm)

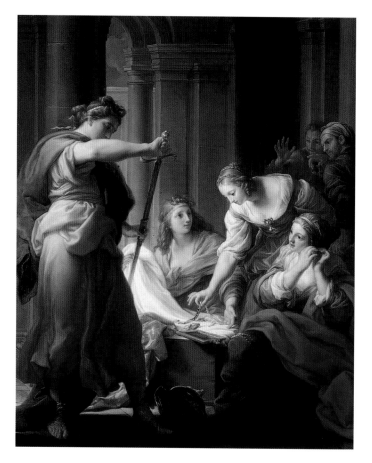

POMPEO BATONI (1708–1787)
Achilles at the Court of Lycomedes, 1745
Oil on canvas, 62 × 49 in. (158.5 × 126.5 cm)

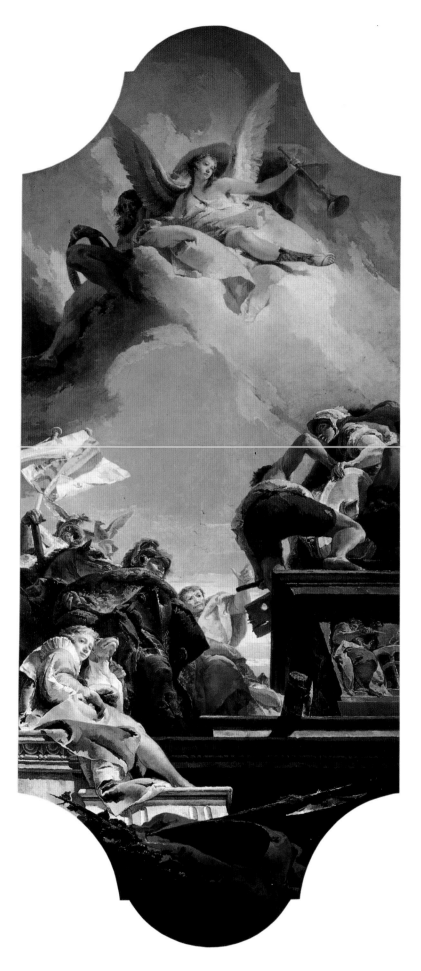

GIOVANNI BATTISTA TIEPOLO (1696–1770)
Erection of a Statue to an Emperor, c. 1730
Oil on canvas, 13 ft. 7 in.× 5 ft. 8¼ in. (4.20 × 1.75 m)

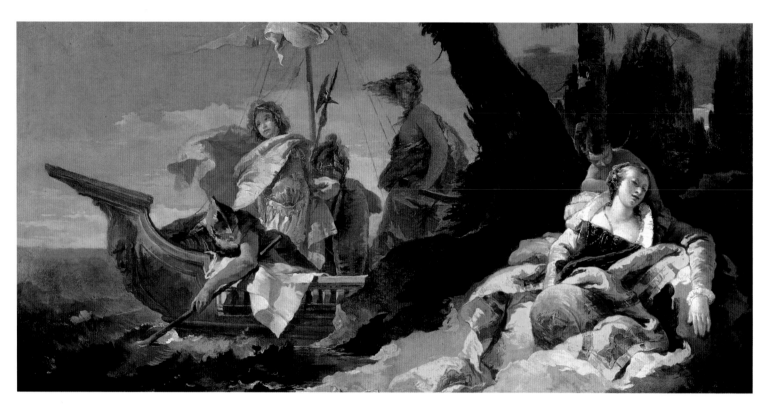

GIOVANNI BATTISTA TIEPOLO (1696–1770)
Rinaldo Abandons Armida, 1750–55
Oil on canvas, 27 × 51½ in. (70 × 132 cm)

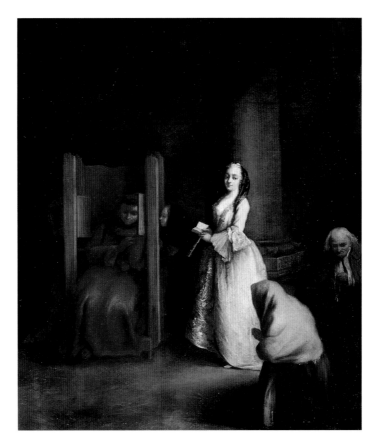

PIETRO LONGHI (1702–1785)
The Confession, c. 1755
Oil on canvas, 23¾ × 19 in. (61 × 49.5 cm)

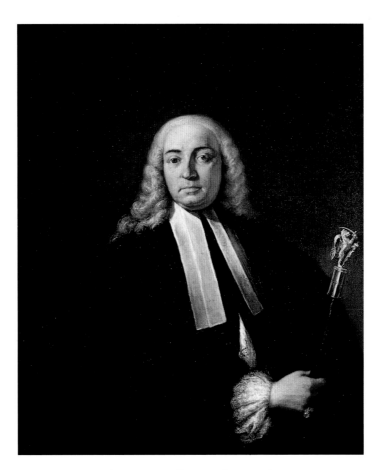

ALESSANDRO LONGHI (1733–1813)
Portrait of a Magistrate, 1780–1800
Oil on canvas, 37 ¾ × 30½ in. (97 × 78 cm)

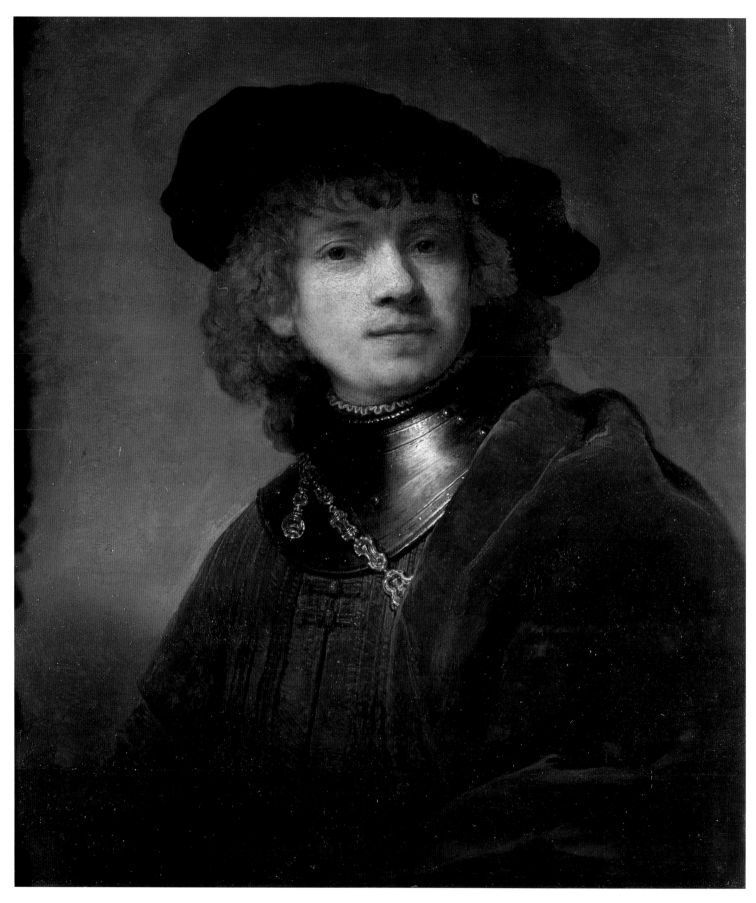

REMBRANDT VAN RIJN (1606–1669)
Self-Portrait as a Young Man, 1634
Oil on canvas, 24¼ × 21 in. (62.5 × 54 cm)

NORTHERN EUROPEAN,
FRENCH, AND
SPANISH PAINTING

DUTCH, FLEMISH, AND GERMAN PAINTING

*T*HE MUSEUM HAS a particularly rich collection from the Dutch, Flemish, and German schools. From the fifteenth century on, Flemish artists in particular were skilled in representing nature and humanity, not subordinating them to any rational principle or intellectual theory but rather employing acute observation in the precise rendering of details—the physical qualities of fabrics, plants, landscapes, and human expressions. The presence of so many Flemish works in Florence indicates their importance to the history of Italian painting, just as northern European artists were influenced by contact with Italian art. An outstanding example of this reciprocal relationship is the great *Portinari Altarpiece* by Hugo van der Goes (page 112), in which the flanking figures in the *Adoration of the Shepherds* are portraits of members of the Florentine Portinari family, who commissioned the work in Bruges. The Portinari were in that city to handle the business interests of the Medici, and when they brought the work home to Florence in 1483 it influenced local painters such as Domenico Ghirlandaio. An example of influence in the opposite direction is *The Entombment* (page 118), painted by Roger van der Weyden in Italy in 1450, which clearly indicates that the Flemish master was familiar with the balanced compositions of contemporary Italian painting. Italian influence is also evident in *The Adoration of the Magi* (page 124), by the German Albrecht Dürer, who also traveled in Italy.

Dürer's beautiful *Portrait of the Artist's Father* (page 125), at once straightforward and affectionate, is displayed together with the more traditional but equally significant portraits by Lucas Cranach, in particular those of Martin Luther and his wife. Cranach's lively and graceful *Adam and Eve* (page 126) must be compared with Hans Baldung Grien's more fluid *Adam and Eve* (page 127): the almost classical proportions of the figures in the latter were based on Dürer.

Hans Memling, whose works had great influence on portrait painting in Tuscany during the fifteenth century, is well represented in the collection. His portraits are characterized by the severe black clothes of his sitters, who are shown half-length, and by the landscape views in the backgrounds.

The seventeenth century was a period of great variety and complexity for European painting, and the Uffizi collection from this period is extensive. During this century the members of the Medici family, from the grand dukes (Cosimo II, Ferdinando II, Cosimo III) to the princes and cardinals, closely followed developments in national and international art and acquired works by the leading artists of each period. Some paintings entered the family collection as gifts or were bought directly in foreign lands, such as the Dutch paintings of which Cosimo III was so fond.

A room in the Uffizi is dedicated to Peter Paul Rubens, who began a close relationship with the Medici during a stay in Italy. In Florence in 1600 he participated in the wedding by proxy of Maria de' Medici to King Henry IV of France. Years later Maria, as queen of France, commissioned him to make an imposing series of large allegorical paintings showing the important events of her life; she later asked for a similar series based on the life of Henry IV. The series was never completed, but two unfinished works in the Uffizi are currently being restored after damage sustained in the May 1993 bombing. Their large size (more than twenty-two feet wide) permitted Rubens, the leading representative of the European Baroque movement, to give full vent to his theatrical and explosive tendencies, using robust and vibrant colors and animated technique. Alongside these official subjects is his portrait of his wife, Isabella Brandt (page 122), which shows how Rubens could direct his talents to other subjects; sensuous affection and playful intimacy run through this warm image of a youthful and vivacious woman. Together with the exuberant works by Rubens are examples of the more reserved and official portraits made by his great pupil Anthony Van Dyck.

The Uffizi's collection of seventeenth-century Dutch painting is rich and varied, but at the moment the museum can display only a small portion of it. There are impressive and moving self-portraits by Rembrandt, and the walls of an entire room are covered with small paintings of various subjects, works of which Cosimo III de' Medici was a passionate collector. Genre scenes painted by Frans van Mieris and Caspar Netscher are displayed together with views by Gerrit Berckeyde and Jacob Ruysdael, and there are also still lifes by Rachel Ruysch and Jan van Huysum. Taken together these works offer a complete panorama of the varied pictorial universe of flourishing bourgeois Holland.

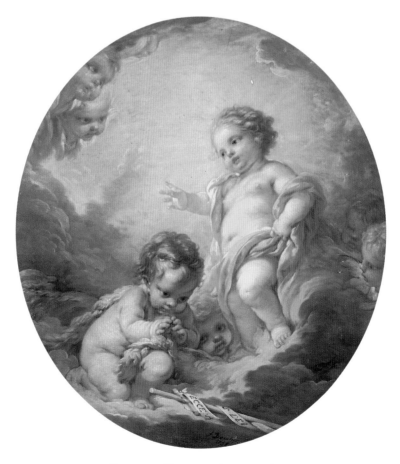

FRANÇOIS BOUCHER (1703–1770)
Christ and John the Baptist as Children, 1758
Oil on oval canvas, 19½ × 17 in. (50 × 44 cm)

FRENCH AND SWISS PAINTING

*G*RAND DUKE Ferdinando III (1769–1824) expanded the Uffizi's collection of French art, acquiring older works in an attempt to match the breadth of the Uffizi's holdings of Italian and Northern art. He also repeatedly sent agents to France to purchase contemporary paintings. As a result, the galleries house an extraordinary selection of French painting from the seventeenth and eighteenth centuries.

Simon Vouet's *Annunciation,* bought in Paris, shows the influence of Caravaggio. The fashion for classical landscapes was best represented in Italy by two French painters, Claude Lorrain and Nicolas Poussin. In Claude's *Port with Villa Medici* (page 134) a "portrait" of the Medici palace in Rome is combined with a fantastic and evocative seaside sunset. Jean-Baptiste-Siméon Chardin's *Girl with Racket and Shuttlecock* (page 136) and *Boy Playing with Cards* (page 136), both ordinary scenes rendered in limpid and luminous tones, give a sense of the heights reached by French artists during the eighteenth century. Elegant official portraits of royal subjects, by Jean-Marc Nattier and others, are contrasted with the astonishingly modern paintings by the Swiss Jean-Etienne Liotard, whose refined *Marie-Adelaide of France in Turkish Dress* (page 137), with its glimpse of a young woman absorbed in her reading, anticipates the intimate tone of nineteenth-century works.

SPANISH PAINTING

*I*T WAS NOT UNTIL late in this century that Spanish works of major importance entered the Uffizi collection. Paintings by Francisco Goya are on display thanks to two relatively recent important acquisitions, including *Maria Theresa of Vallabriga on Horseback* (page 142), with its unusual and powerful color combinations, and *The Countess of Chinchon* (page 142), remarkable for both its delicate and respectful psychological study and the masterful technique used to render the pearly dress and feathered headdress. Another important acquisition of the 1970s was a painting by El Greco, *Saints John the Evangelist and Francis* (page 139).

The Contini Bonacossi donation came to the Uffizi in 1974, bringing a version of the celebrated *Water Carrier of Seville* by Velázquez (page 140) to complement two works by Velázquez in the self-portrait collection—one of which entered the collection as early as 1690. The Contini Bonacossi donation also includes a Torero attributed to Goya; The Tears of Saint Peter, a splendid work by El Greco; and *Saint Anthony Abbot* by Francisco de Zurbarán (page 141).

DUTCH PAINTING

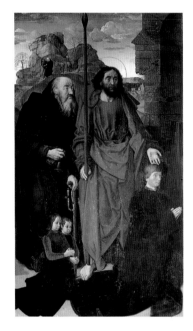
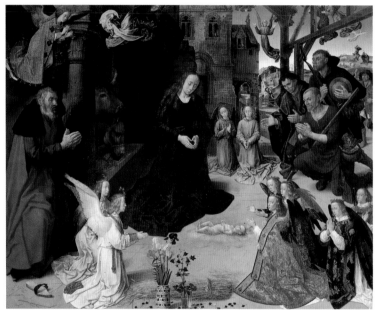
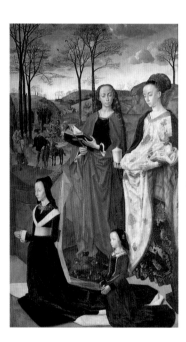

Hugo van der Goes (c. 1440–1482)
Portinari Altarpiece
(The Adoration of the Shepherds), c. 1475
Oil on wood, 8 ft. 2½ in. × 18 ft. 5 in. (2.53 × 5.68 m) overall

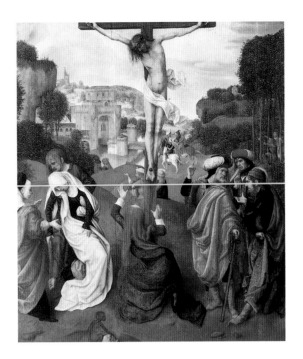

MASTER OF THE VIRGO INTER VIRGINES (active c. 1460–1520)
The Crucifixion, n.d.
Oil on wood, 22¼ × 18¼ in. (57 × 47 cm)

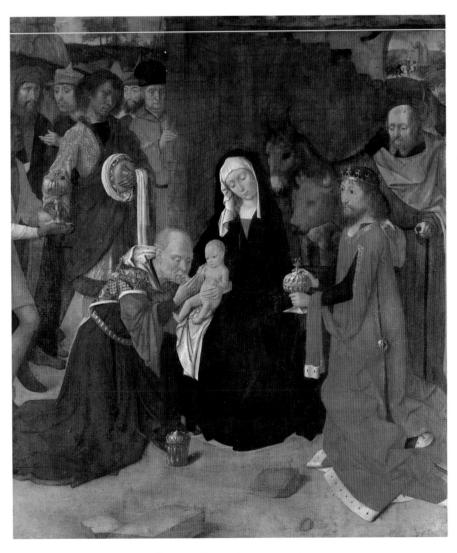

GERARD DAVID (c. 1460–1523)
The Adoration of the Magi, c. 1490
Watercolor on canvas, 37 × 31 in. (95 × 80 cm)

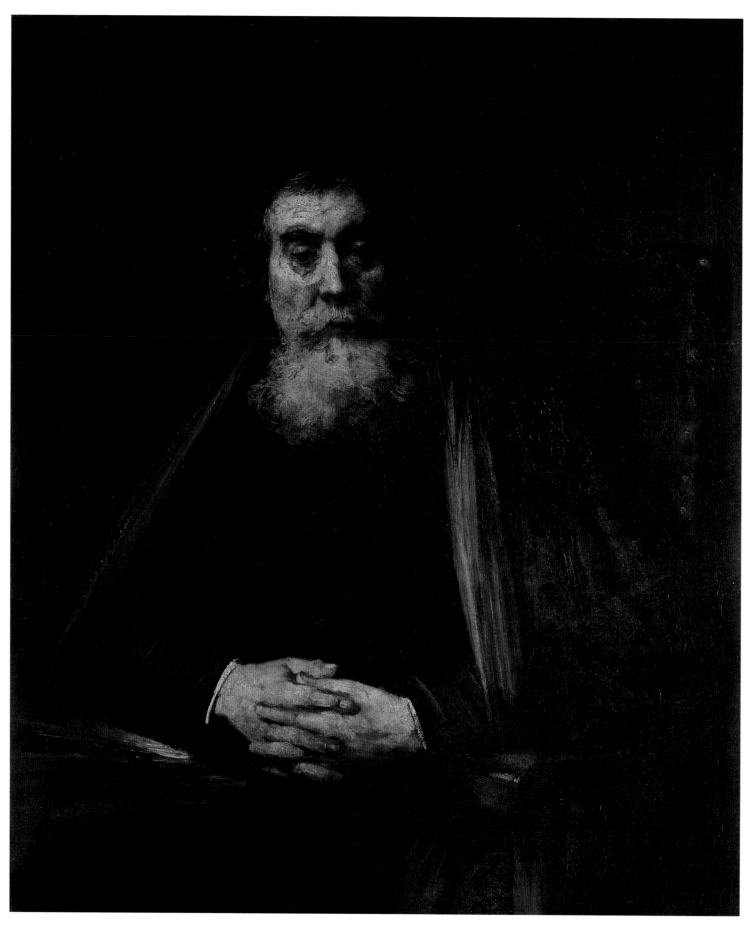

REMBRANDT VAN RIJN (1606–1669)
Portrait of an Old Man, 1665
Oil on canvas, 40½ × 33½ in. (104 × 86 cm)

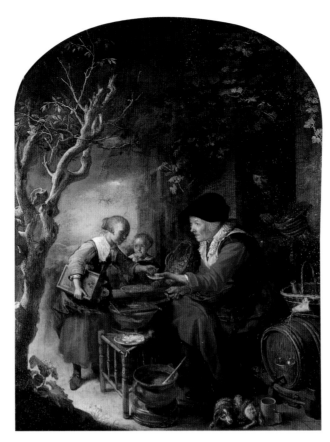

GERARD DOU (1613–1675)
Pancake Seller, 1650–55
Oil on wood, 17 × 13¼ in. (44 × 34 cm)

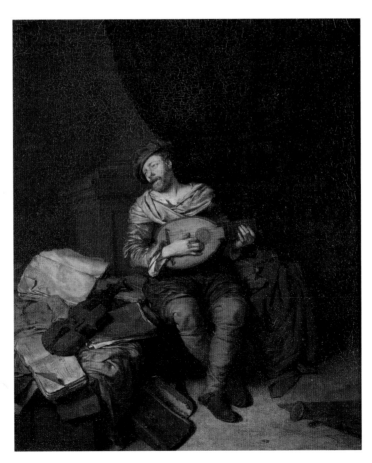

CORNELIS BEGA (1631/32–1664)
Guitar Player, 1664
Oil on wood, 14 × 12½ in. (36 × 32 cm)

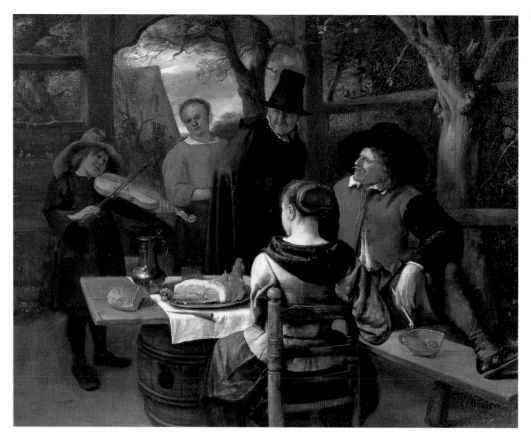

JAN STEEN (1626–1679)
The Luncheon, 1650–60
Oil on wood, 16 × 19½ in. (41 × 49.5 cm)

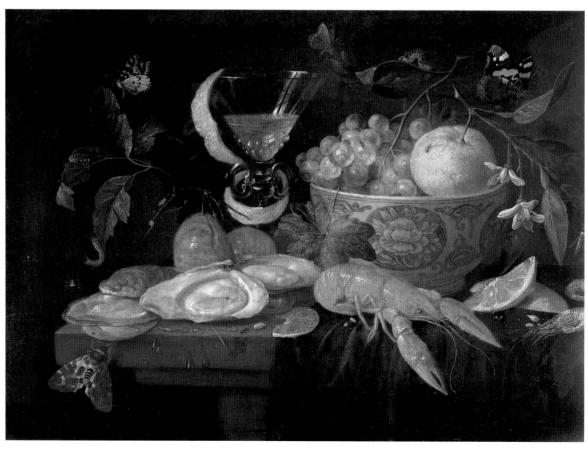

JAN VAN KESSEL (1626–1679)
Still Life with Fruit and Shellfish, 1653
Oil on canvas, 12 × 17 in. (31 × 44 cm)

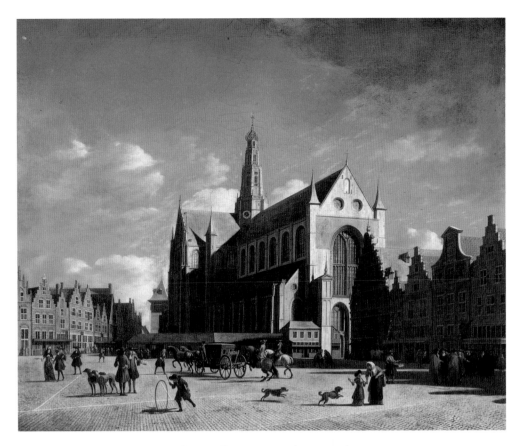

GERRIT BERCKHEYDE (1638–1698)
The Market at Haarlem, 1693
Oil on canvas, 21 × 25 in. (54 × 64 cm)

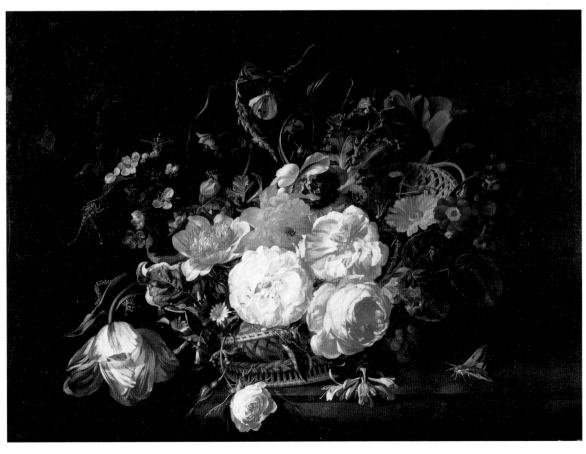

RACHEL RUYSCH (1664–1750)
Flowers and Insects, 1711
Oil on wood, 17 × 25¾ in. (44 × 66 cm)

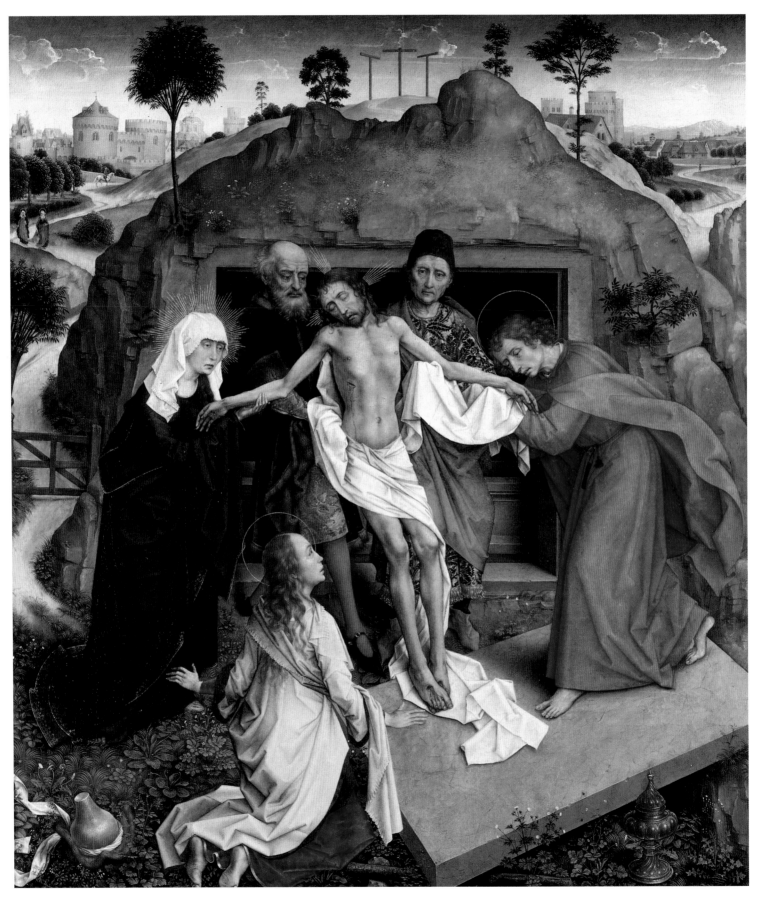

ROGER VAN DER WEYDEN (c. 1400–1464)
The Entombment, 1450
Oil on canvas, 43 × 37¾ in. (110 × 96 cm)

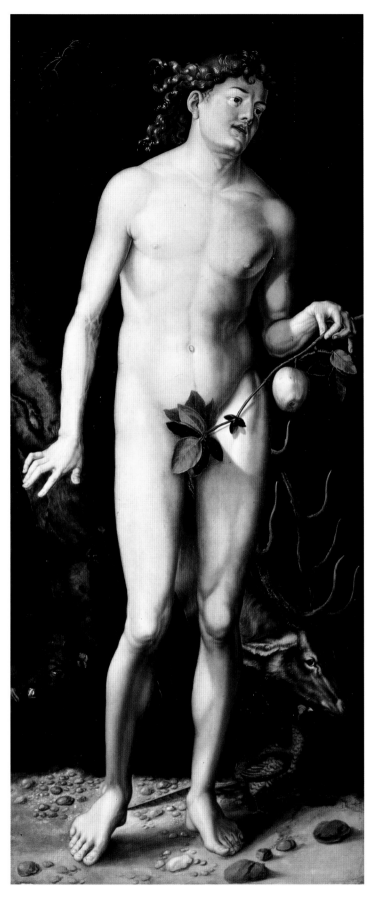

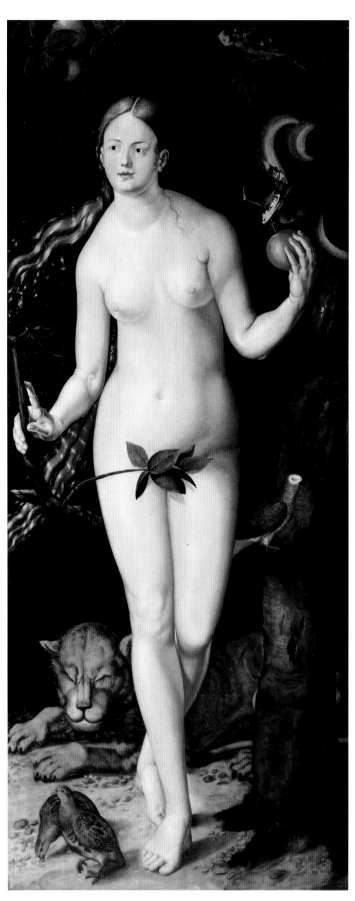

HANS BALDUNG GRIEN (c. 1484–1545)
Adam (after Dürer), c. 1507
Oil on wood, 82½ × 33 in. (212 × 85 cm)

HANS BALDUNG GRIEN (c. 1484–1545)
Eve (after Dürer), c. 1507
Oil on wood, 82½ × 33 in. (212 × 85 cm)

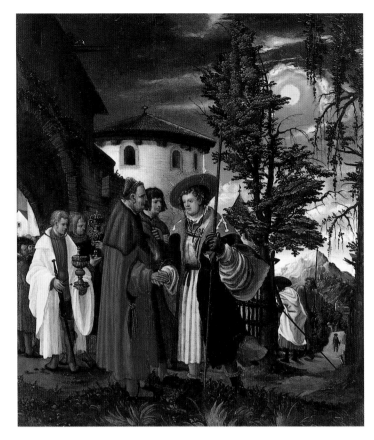

ALBRECHT ALTDORFER (1480–1538)
The Departure of Saint Florian, c. 1520
Oil on wood, 31¾ × 26 in. (81.4 × 67 cm)

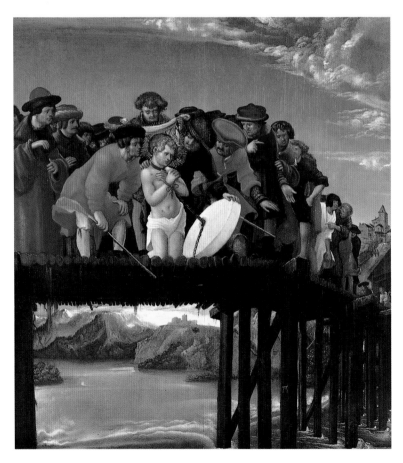

ALBRECHT ALTDORFER (1480–1538)
The Martyrdom of Saint Florian, c. 1520
Oil on wood, 29¾ × 26¼ in. (76.4 × 67.2 cm)

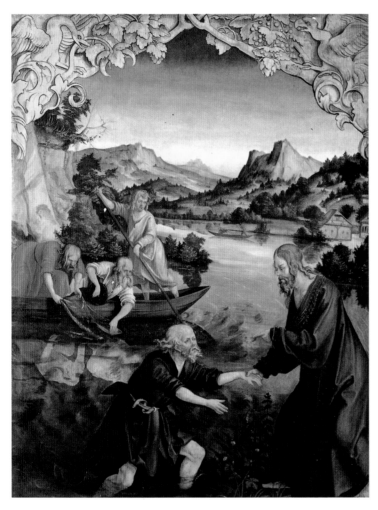

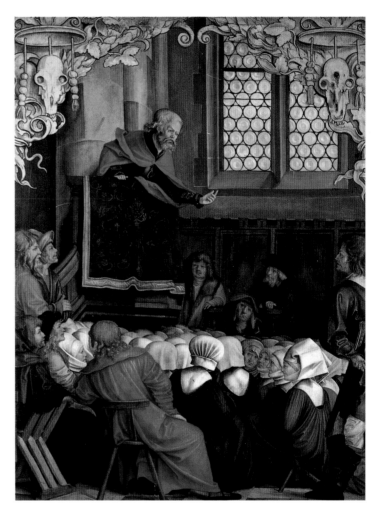

HANS VON KULMBACH (c. 1480–1522)
The Calling of Saint Peter, 1514–16
Oil on wood, 50⅝ × 37¼ in. (128.5 × 95.5 cm)

HANS VON KULMBACH (c. 1480–1522)
The Sermon of Saint Peter, 1514–16
Oil on wood, 51⅛ × 37¼ in. (130 × 95.5 cm)

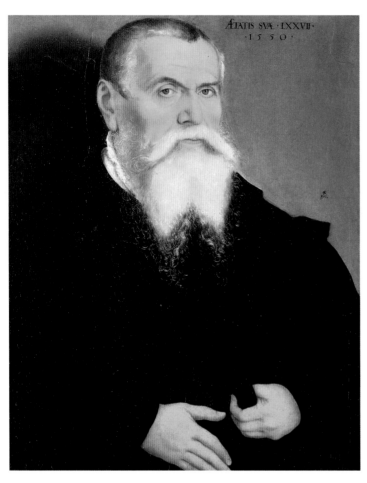

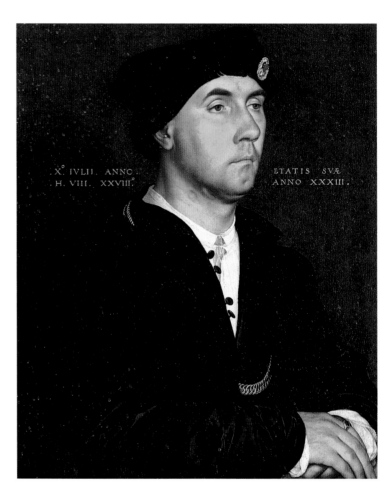

LUCAS CRANACH THE YOUNGER (1515–1586)
Lucas Cranach the Elder, 1550
Oil on wood, 25 × 19 in. (64 × 49 cm)

HANS HOLBEIN THE YOUNGER (c. 1497–1543)
Sir Richard Southwell, 1536
Oil on wood, 18½ × 15 in. (47.5 × 38 cm)

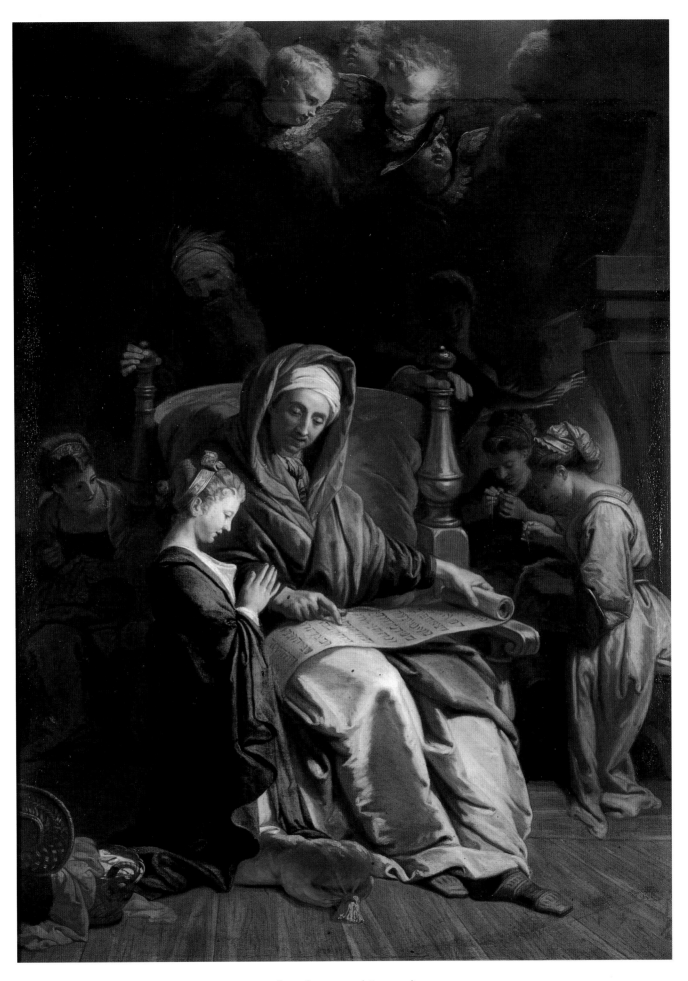

JEAN JOUVENET (1644–1717)
The Education of the Virgin, 1700
Oil on canvas, 39¾ × 27½ in. (102 × 71 cm)

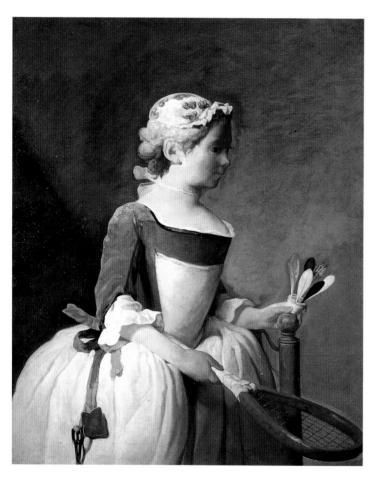

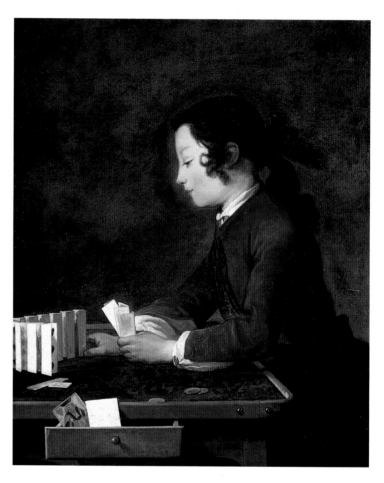

JEAN-BAPTISTE-SIMÉON CHARDIN (1699–1779)
Girl with Racket and Shuttlecock, c. 1740
Oil on canvas, 32 × 25¾ in. (82 × 66 cm)

JEAN-BAPTISTE-SIMÉON CHARDIN (1699–1779)
Boy Playing with Cards, c. 1740
Oil on canvas, 32 × 25¾ in. (82 × 66 cm)

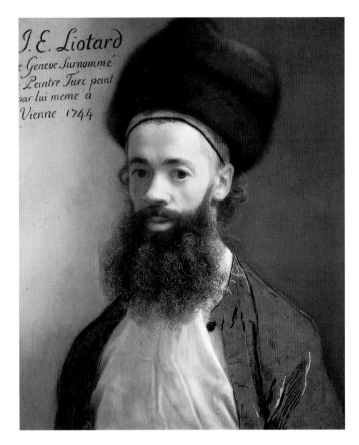

JEAN-ETIENNE LIOTARD (1702–1789)
Self-Portrait, n.d.
Pastel on paper, 23¾ × 19 in. (61 × 49 cm)

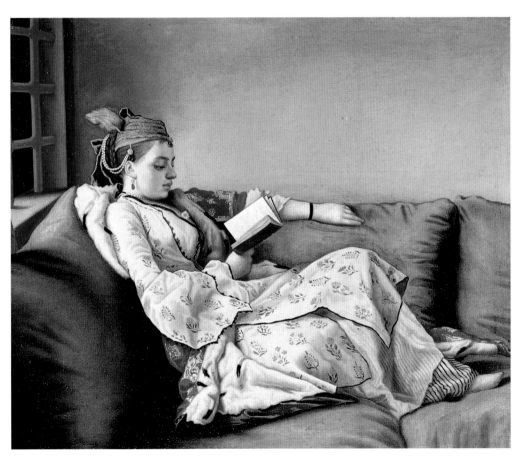

JEAN-ETIENNE LIOTARD (1702–1789)
Marie-Adelaide of France in Turkish Dress, 1753
Oil on canvas, 19½ × 22 in. (50 × 56 cm)

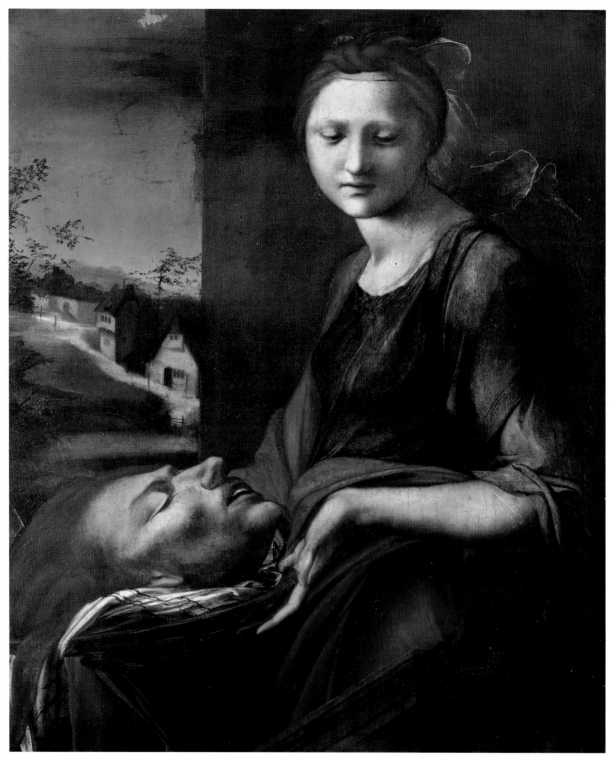

ALONSO BERRUGUETE (1488–1561)
Salome, 1512/16
Oil on wood, 34 × 27½ in. (87.5 × 71 cm)

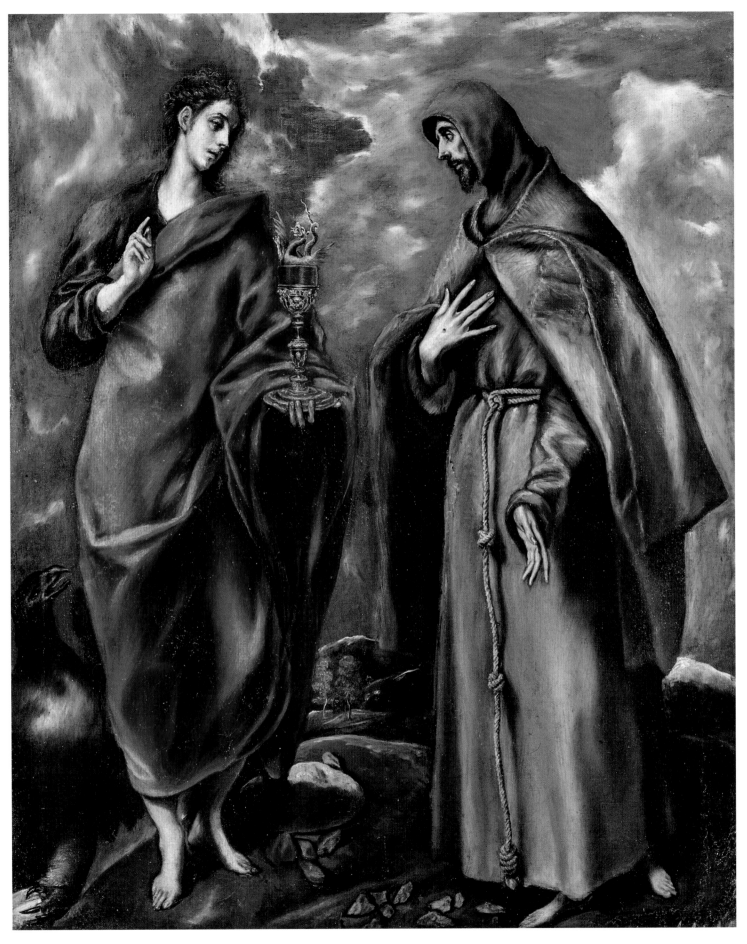

EL GRECO (1541–1614)
Saints John the Evangelist and Francis, c. 1600
Oil on canvas, 43 x 33½ in. (110 x 86 cm)

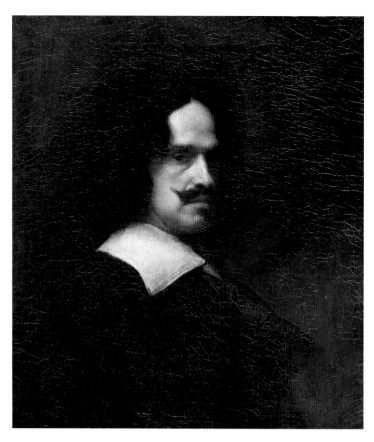

DIEGO VELÁZQUEZ (1599–1660)
Self-Portrait, c. 1643
Oil on canvas, 40¼ × 32 in. (103.5 × 82.5 cm)

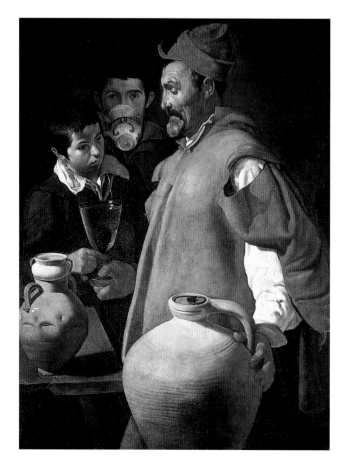

DIEGO VELÁZQUEZ (1599–1660)
The Water Carrier of Seville, c. 1620
Oil on canvas, 40½ × 29¼ in. (104 × 75 cm)

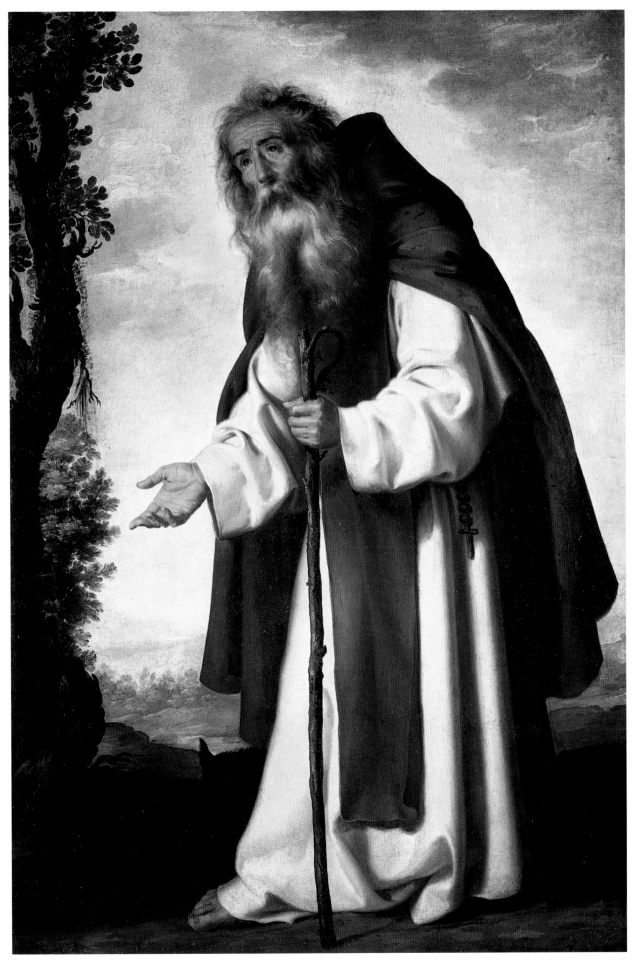

FRANCISCO DE ZURBARÁN (1598–1664)
Saint Anthony Abbot, c. 1640
Oil on canvas, 69 × 45½ in. (177 × 117 cm)

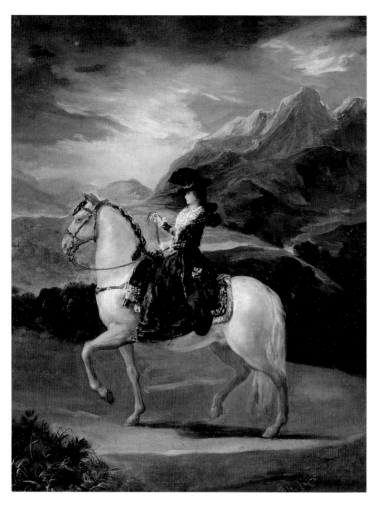

FRANCISCO DE GOYA (1746–1828)
Maria Theresa of Vallabriga on Horseback, 1783
Oil on canvas, 32 × 24 in. (82.5 × 61.7 cm)

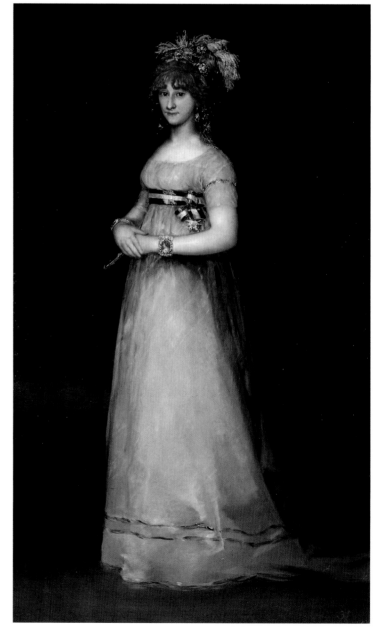

FRANCISCO DE GOYA (1746–1828)
The Countess of Chinchon, c. 1801
Oil on canvas, 86 × 55 in. (220 × 140 cm)

INDEX OF ILLUSTRATIONS